OYIBOS

Memoirs of Culture Shock

GUS UDO

Copyright © 2011 by Augustine F. Udo

All rights reserved. No part of this publication may be reproduced or transmitted in any form or by any means, electronic or mechanical, including photocopy, recording, or any information storage and retrieval system, without permission in writing from the publisher.

Requests for permission to make copies of any part of the work should be submitted to: gusudo@gusudo.com.

Oyibos: Memoirs of Culture Shock/Gus Udo

1. Memoirs-Biography. 2. Immigrants-United States-England. 3. Africa-Nigeria-Ibos-Biafra. 4. Harvard. 5. New York. I. Title.

ISBN: 978-0-9840453-1-0
eISBN 978-0-9840453-0-3

Printed in the United States

First Edition

Family Tree

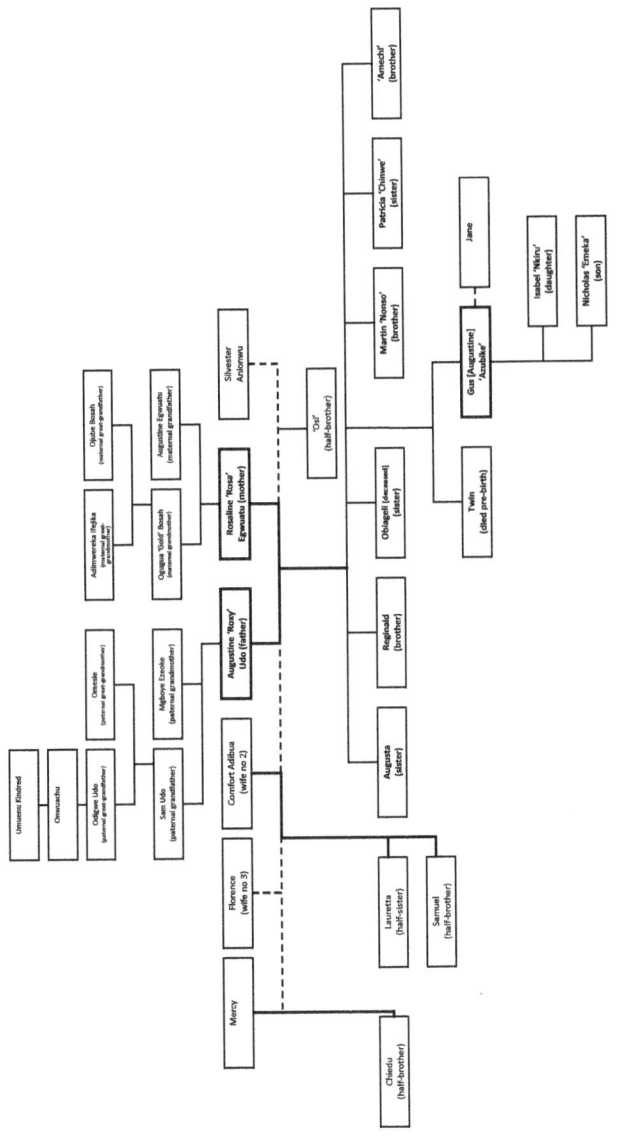

CONTENT

PART I: Escape: 1959-1966 1
1. Dangerous Situation...3
2. Early Years..7
3. London...27
4. Wessex Gardens..39
5. Biafra 46

PART II: The Green Belt: 1966-1979 55
6. The Real World 57
7. Dollis..65
8. John Holt..71
9. Finchley..80
10. Sports and Athletics 91
11. Lagos 101

PART III: New Pastures: 1979-Present 115
12. Harvard 117
13. London School of Economics and Political Science (LSE)...139
14. Love and Lehman..144
15. Manhattan 156
16. Work and Adventure 161
17. Uncompromising Friendship 177
18. Building Bridges..183
19. The Burial..192
20. Failed Dreams...198

EPILOGUE...................................223

Onitsha.....................................224

Acknowledgements 232
Suggested Reading 233
Author's Biography...235

Chronology

Key background Events

800 BC: Nok civilization in Jos plateau.

1472: Portuguese navigate Nigerian coastline.

1500: Migration of Onitsha settlers from Benin.

1857: Arrival of first British traders in Onitsha.

1886: Queen Victoria grants Royal Niger Company trading charter.

1900: Transfer of administration of Onitsha from Royal Nigeria Company to the British Crown.

1928: Father born (his date).

1927: First colonial tax revenues collected.

1932: Mother born.

1951: Parent's marriage.

1956: Death of Obiageli and paternal grandmother.

1959: Born; same birthday as "Zik".

1960: October 1, Nigerian Independence from Britain.

1962/63: National census ignites ethnic and regional tensions.

1963/64: Father permanently posted to London, England.

1965: Started school in Lagos, Nigeria.

1966:
- January, first military coup in Nigeria; July, counter-coup.
- July/August, we flee to Onitsha and return to Lagos.

- September, family escapes to London on holiday.
- September, pogrom of Ibos in northern Nigeria.
- October, siblings and mother return to Lagos.
- December, mother and siblings return to London.

1967/70: Biafra secedes; Biafra-Nigeria Civil War.

1967/69: Attended Wessex Garden Primary School.

1969: Family moves to Mill Hill from Golders Green.

1969/72: Attended Dollis Primary School.

1972/79: Attended Finchley Catholic High School for Boys.

1978: Competed in athletics for Great Britain Juniors.

1979/83: Attended Harvard College.

1979/90: Margaret Thatcher, UK Prime Minister.

1983/84: Attended London School of Economics & Political Science.

1985: Commenced work at Shearson Lehman Brothers, New York.

1988: Founded International Asset Transactions.

1991: Met Jane in New York.

1993: Became a Naturalized American.

1996: Isabel born; death of my maternal grandmother.

2004: Jane's mother dies; father dies in December.

2006: Nicholas born.

2008: Separation from Jane.

2009: Wrote first book.

In memory of my father
and dedicated to my mother and children

"There is no wealth but life" — John Ruskin

OYIBOS

Memoirs of Culture Shock

PART I: Escape: 1959-1966

1. Dangerous Situation

> "When our parents invite us to come and join them on earth they forget to inform us of all the twists and turns the journey will take." - Nigerian saying.

Six years old, clasping my eyes and ears in terror, I huddled closer and clung desperately to my screaming mother in the backseat of our electric-blue Peugeot. I braced myself for the furious sound of a machine gun burst, when suddenly my two younger siblings began to sob uncontrollably. Their innocent voices and the sight of tears falling from their angelic faces momentarily quelled the tension. The previously agitated check-point soldier looked up and smiled; he eased his finger off the trigger and lowered the butt of his weapon to rest in the pool of bright yellow urine which surrounded him and Godwin, our driver. He was told to wave us through by his commanding officer, who stood in the heat haze. "I de go" (I'm going), he said calmly. Attention now shifted to the large over-laden truck behind us full of fellow fleeing Ibos whose fate we would not know. Danger for now had been averted, at least for us. Godwin, who a moment earlier was about to be shot, picked himself off the wet asphalt and stepped back into the driver's seat, accompanied by the heavy odor of urine and adrenaline-laced perspiration. The Peugeot accelerated away. Terrified we looked back intently through the rear windscreen at the hastily contrived check-point made of oil drums, burnt tires, and tufts

Dangerous Situation

of bush-grass. We saw a phalanx of lean, tall, dark unruly Hausa soldiers violently dragging off weeping men. Their voices shrill with terror, begging for mercy, "Don Allah!" (Please!), "I beg", as they disappeared into the bush.

This is one of my most vivid early childhood memories of Nigeria. This single event changed my and my family's destiny forever and our connection to an amazing country that I still feel remarkable attachment to even after growing up in England, and living in America for almost 30 years.

As with many uprooted immigrants, I've waged the battle of identity and survival, to hold onto who I am despite a journey through three continents and cultures. More often than not I have foreign currency (Euro, Naira, and Pounds) in my pockets, as well as a New York subway metro card, London tube Oyster Card, and Paris Metro carnet tickets, symbols of my life across three continents and countries with differing cultures, none of which I fully belong to. I am borderless although not stateless, since an American can be many different things as I discovered at my citizenship swearing-in ceremony in downtown Manhattan in 1993. Those present were of all hues: black, white, yellow and all shades in between. Some wore turbans, others wore headscarves, and I may have even seen someone in Dutch clogs. The large municipal hall was filled as the witty but respectful judge asked us to raise our right-hands to pledge allegiance to the United States and to foreswear all and any allegiances to foreign potentates.

It was only one of many journeys that would take me from a polygamous household in a teaming city on the brink of an explosive civil war, to a council house in Thatcher England, from an all boys' Catholic school to the hallowed halls of Harvard, from a jarring initiation to a Wall Street career to the culture shock of an American home life. These journeys would take me away from who I thought I was, to what I became, always raising questions along the way about what it means to be Onitsha-Ibo, a Nigerian, British, an Ivy Leaguer, and an American.

In unison with the colorful assembly of aspirant Americans gathered in the courtroom, I answered: "Yes!" I was now an American, freshly minted like a shining new silver dollar coin. I surveyed the scene of spontaneous jubilation and pondered the stories of others standing beside me. What were their journeys? What stories lay untold in their minds and smiling faces? What was the future for all of us? We left the hall, like many generations of Americans before us, with our otherness, the separation that marked us apart as outsiders, at least symbolically for now, disconnected by the force of law.

My previously animated heart grew quiet. I stepped outside and inhaled deeply. I felt the invigorating icy breeze of New York's East River on my face. I flashed back in time and was moved by harrowing memories of our escape in late 1966 from impending civil war. I was at the frontier between the second and the third act in my tri-cultural existence. America beckoned with its promise of freedom and a better life. Like the startling realization of a geometric proof, what was now certain was that I would not be fighting any wars for Nigeria or any other foreign potentates. Nor would I bear a British passport, like my parents sometimes talked about, as part of the cadre of fabled British-Africans who have scaled the country's art, literary, sports, and other professional ranks. What was less obvious was the depth and

Dangerous Situation

strength of my lingering cultural and spiritual ties, which would not be broken so easily.

2. Early Years

I asked Bolaji in Yoruba: "Why do they hate Ibos", and he shrugged his shoulders with the look of innocence and said: "I don't hate you."

Despite the uproar around us, my pretty diminutive mother, a strict disciplinarian, tried to maintain calm in our household. She ruled us firmly with an iron fist or foot as more commonly was the case during my father's long absence while he was posted to London. My siblings and I referred to her special disciplinarian technique as "unzobu unzubo" which loosely translates in Ibo to: "to stamp (or stomp) upon with one's feet". She was struggling to cope with five young children and our two cousins Okey and Theresa who were strong willed and independent teenagers. Theresa's stunning beauty, like that of certain other Udo women in the fullness of their youth (one of my first cousins would later be crowned Miss Nigeria), attracted endless unsuitable suitors, principally non-Onitsha indigenes, individuals considered of doubtful social origin who were treated as foreigners and had to be seen-off. Sometimes even Oyibos (Europeans) touched by the sun and eager to go native.

I was six years-old and it was strange I thought being in the midst of people who wanted you dead. We lived in Lagos, the heart of enemy territory, and if it had not been for the love and protection of our Yoruba neighbors who shielded us from hostile Federal soldiers, we would not be alive today. Although our parents spoke Ibo to us, we all had become very proficient in Yoruba which was the predominant language in Lagos. Plurilingual, we were at various points in time conversant in Ibo, Hausa, and Yoruba. Many of our friends, like the Rotibi's, were Yoruba. Mr.

Early Years

Rotibi was a very prosperous oil services distributor for Shell. The arrival of the oil giants in Nigeria in the fifties brought with it the welcome seeds of American cultural imperialism through television. The Rotibi children and my siblings moved between our houses like one home, particularly on nights when Bonanza or Sergeant Bilko were on television and the whole neighborhood would gather to watch through their open first floor louver windows. That is until the power failed and the neighbors scattered to their homes with torches, Calor Gas or kerosene lamps. Neighborhoods in those days were generally safe and village-like, even in urban Lagos. Our street was watched over by fearsome Hausa "Maigadi" night watchmen.

Bolaji Rotibi was my best friend and we were inseparable. We moved inconspicuously and anonymously in Lagos, a bubbling caldron which attracted people from all corners of Nigeria and beyond.

As tensions escalated, mother was finally forced to evacuate us from Lagos along with thousands of other terrified Ibos. She fled with her children and all our belongings back to Onitsha in eastern Nigeria. The scene was chaotic and tense. Our Yoruba neighbors implored my mother to stay, assuring her that all would be safe; but it was difficult to know where friendship remained and perilous ethnic enmity lay hidden. Frantic confused goodbyes were said to my childhood friends. Bolaji like me was equally bewildered by the swirling and sudden changes in previously cordial social arrangements. Neighbors became unexplained foes overnight and innocent childhood play became impossible.

En route to Onitsha, we navigated dangerous roadblocks and check-points manned by trigger-happy northern troops seeking fleeing foot-soldiers and their officers with tell-tale black or camouflage military boots on their feet. On arrival in the safe-haven of Onitsha, we unloaded all our worldly belongings. Rosa, my stunned exhausted mother, was then promptly ordered to leave immediately for London to the bosom of her husband, by my father's playful elder brother. Uncle Simon (Obi), told my mother to have Roxy, my father, send airline tickets with haste. This was his entitlement as a senior Airways official, although there was some debate whether he had exhausted his quota on tickets for Comfort, his second wife. Simon was my father's beloved brother and he understood that if we were not rushed from Nigeria that the family was likely to be slaughtered or perish in the ensuing wave of conflict. Mother now had the daunting task of retracing her escape route through the same perilous gauntlet of soldiers and dangerous roadblocks, since Lagos's Ikeja airport was the only gateway for commercial flights out of the country.

As expected of someone of my father's station, he owned property both in Mainland Onitsha, and our ancestral village in the Umu Dei quarter of the town. There are sixteen Ogbe (quarters) in Onitsha and historically all members of an Ogbe are blood related, being descended from the same paternal line. Accordingly, my father had commissioned a house built in our family ogbe and another built by Italian engineers with lustrous imported marble atop a hill in a secluded ogbe. As was my father's want, this house was well situated off the Awka Road but was not in the highly desired GRA (Government Reserved Area) which housed the ruling white colonials. The house was bombed and looted when the war was at its height and family heirlooms, which my mother had carefully transported from Lagos, including family picture albums were taken away. After innocently requesting a cigarette from one of his colonial bosses, uncle Simon, who was living in the house, lost his "Olu Oyibo" (work in the colonial administration and other related private businesses operated by Europeans, as opposed to "Olu Obodo", work within the realm of the local community) with AG Leventis, a trading company founded by a prominent Cypriot businessman. He was shot dead by Federal troops for refusing to surrender the house which he was tending until our return. The task of rebuilding was supervised by my Aunt Josephine in my father's absence once the war was over.

Like many Nigerian families, our family destiny was profoundly altered by the Nigeria-Biafra Civil War of 1967 to 1970. The origins of Nigeria's civil war are complex and are best understood in the context of the country's colonial history. Nigeria is comprised of about 300 different ethnic and tribal groups many with differing languages and customs. English is the official lingua franca, although Pidgin English, a blend of English and local languages is more widely spoken. The country is dominated by three ethnic groups: the Hausa-Fulani in the northern part of the country, the Yoruba in the West, and the Ibos in the East. During the period of colonial control, the British governed Nigeria indirectly employing a "divide and rule system"; the favored feudal autocratic Muslim north was largely isolated from Western religious and educational encroachment and as a result trailed its southern Ibo and Yoruba counterparts in terms of Western academic scholarship. It was the Ibo and Yoruba dominated parties led by Western educated elites Awolowo and Zik that were at the vanguard of the Independence Movement, leaving some northerners fearful of southern domination. Southerners already controlled commerce, Nigeria's civil service and the officer ranks of the armed forces to the extent that the British found it necessary ahead of Independence to introduce quotas to right these imbalances and to assist the advancement of northerners. This prevailing colonial system intensified ethnic and tribal tensions which were fanned by the country's political leaders jockeying for control of the reins of power.

Post-Independence tensions were high and the country with each passing year was drifting perilously toward fragmentation along the lines of the three dominant ethnic and tribal groups. The botched 1962-3 census and crisis surrounding electoral irregularities in the 1965 elections, and the northern pogroms culminated in a coup led by junior officers on January 15, 1966. General Johnson Aguiyi-Ironsi an Ibo emerged as the country's first military President. The coup plotters cited corrupt and inept civilian government as their motive. Northerners perceived the coup as an Ibo coup; a northern led counter-coup followed by Lieutenant Colonel Murtala Muhammed on July 29, 1966. General Ironsi and many senior Ibo military officers and rank-and-file troops were killed. In September 1966, a large-scale massacre of Christian Ibos by northern Muslims ensued in the North that saw tens of thousands slaughtered and maimed. Ironsi was replaced by the Sandhurst trained Lieutenant Colonel Yakubu Gowon, a northern Christian who attempted to restore order and to forestall civil war. A mass exodus of almost 2 million Ibos followed from the North to their home towns and villages in the East. Talks aimed at reaching a compromise peace accord among the leaders of the North, West, and East failed, and the military Governor of the East, Oxford educated son of a trucking millionaire Colonel Chukwuemeka Odumegwu Ojukwu declared secession from Nigeria under the Republic of Biafra on May 30, 1967, citing the pogroms and electoral fraud as provocation. War soon commenced on July 6, 1967, when Nigerian Federal troops advanced into Biafra.

Biafra surrendered on January 13, 1970, at Amichi, my paternal grandmother's hometown, Colonel Ojukwu having fled in exile to the Ivory Coast or Côte d'Ivoire as it is now known.

My mother was my father's first wife; one of three he took under local custom in his lifetime. Polygamy was common even among Christians. They had seven children of whom six survived. He was her second union. My mother had already given birth to my half-brother Osi before marrying my father. Osi was the product of a relationship with a local civil servant who my mother left after my father proposed marriage and completed customary marriage rites. This included several visits which gave each of the two families an opportunity to get to know each other and to assess their respective households to ensure the suitability of the match.

Following the birth of my sister Augusta and my brother Regi, was the birth of my sister, the cheerful and beautiful Obiageli, born on December 15, 1956. She died of complications from measles at fifteen months, a year before my birth. Another, my twin (ejima), was lost before birth. These losses were very painful for my parents. All family pictures of Obiageli, except for one my mother kept, were removed, leaving a blank where her smiling framed face once stood. The death of my paternal grandmother, a local princess, who my father adored, in the same year, was a further blow. This trilogy of loss left a profound cloud of sorrow in our home.

When we were in Enugu, before being posted to Lagos, my long suffering mother would on some days find her trousseau tossed out on the street, which was distressing for us her children but was not an uncommon practice when a husband and wife quarreled. She showed my father great forbearance, and her possessions were back in the house by the time we woke the next morning which made us happy once more. Enugu marked a watershed for the family and a change in direction in my father's quest for marital bliss when he took a second wife; but more on this later. First let me tell you about my father.

Known then by his Ibo name Onnua, he was an accomplished athletic tennis player and got on well with his white colonial mentors who quickly recognized his talent and intellect. He was chosen by the colonial administration to train in England in the late fifties before Nigeria's Independence in 1960. After completing high school, my father was invited to Kano in northern Nigeria to live with his uncle and soon gained employment in the colonial civil service. He subsequently landed a plum position with the West African Airways Corporation (WAAC) the forerunner to Nigeria Airways and was posted for an extended period in Kano and Kaduna in northern Nigeria where I was born. Father's rapid advance earned him the playful "U2 Can Fly" moniker among his friends. He had spent time in the North as a youth and spoke Hausa fluently. This was the dominant language there. He was also fluent in his native tongue (Onitsha) Ibo and English. His favorite Hausa saying was: An Wanke Tukwu Nye Don Gobe (wash your pot [plate], because tomorrow you will need it); this fluency in Hausa would serve him well in dealing with the Hausa-Fulani aristocratic dynasty that assumed the mantle of wealth and power in Nigeria after the civil war. He rose quickly through the ranks to become the highest ranking local employee of WAAC, and after postings in Enugu in eastern Nigeria, the family eventually settled in Lagos the then national capital and largest commercial center.

Though I was very young when the family lived in northern Nigeria in the ancient Muslim towns of Kano and Kaduna in the late-fifties and early-sixties, I sensed that my father's fondest memories were in this arid and dry Muslim region with its ancient culture and customs. The family enjoyed a comfortable life in Kano and Kaduna. Like other newly anointed indigenous senior civil servant families, we lived in a large well-appointed bungalow spacious enough to accommodate a growing family and a stream of visiting kinsfolk, a gardener to maintain the lush tropical flower beds, houseboy (Yusufu) who kept my father's uniform pressed and starched with epaulets firmly in place, and driver. As was custom, my father eagerly contributed to and funded the education of many relatives, even at times to his and the family's detriment. He also had two Alsatian dogs, Bingo and Whiskey who stayed close to their master. Other privileges I am told by my elder siblings Augusta and Regi included ponies and riding lessons, private tutors, as well as garden parties, cocktails, Polo Club, Durbar horse parades and lawn tennis; basically all the privileges and peculiar distractions that denoted the eccentricities of English colonial life at the twilight of Britain's imperial power. Nigeria's Durbar was modeled after the ceremonial pageantry of those in India. Under the Raj during the days of the British Empire glistening precious jeweled gifts were lavished on the assembled British brass at the Durbar. The country's first Durbar was organized in Kano in 1925 in honor of Prince Edward, the son of King George the V's State visit to Nigeria. This comfortable and privileged legacy was one that would prove difficult to replicate or indeed to surpass generationally for us his children.

Our stint in the North was a distant cry from the hassle and bustle that greeted us in metropolitan Lagos which would become our home in the early-sixties. On arrival, we lived briefly in a compact flat above the Nigeria Airways offices in Apapa before settling in Shackleford Street (which for reasons that remain unclear, was later renamed Patience Street) in a modest neighborhood in Mainland Lagos. I recall playing on the upstairs veranda of Airways House with its open lattice work and my mother fretting that we might tumble down to the driveway below like baby birds from a nest. For reasons that were best known by my father he eschewed posh areas like Victoria Island and Ikoyi where many of his peers lived for more down-to-earth neighborhoods.

My father was permanently posted to London in 1964 after several training visits. He left us in Lagos with my mother and I was sad to see him go. I wished he would have stayed so that I could at least have an opportunity to know him. My memories of my father at the time were of a handsome athletic playful man, who had a rose-water fragrance after his shower and wore a white string singlet with a native wrapper. We watched father longingly pack and unpack a fat bulging soft black leather suit holdall which contained: mothballs, several tailored suits, shirts, ties, starched pressed underwear, shoes, and a large leather fold-out toiletry bag with a mechanical razor, Wilkinson sword blades, shaving brush, and alum for soothing cuts and razor burn. This was a year after the birth of my pretty stylish sister Chibougwu (God is medicine) (Patricia) or Chinwe as she is known within the family. My father did visit on his long-leaves from London where he headed the overseas operations of the country's national carrier, Nigeria Airways. He brought with him amazing gifts, toy dolls with strange golden hair, a motorized Bentley you could drive with electric lights and pneumatic tires from London's famous Hamleys Toy Shop. These extravagant gifts were the envy of the neighborhood children and were usually reduced to ruin within forty-eight hours of rigorous use by the neighborhood kids. After which we contented ourselves with playing with Nigeria Airways decks of cards and complimentary paper fans with magical sounding cities and destinations like Rio and Singapore.

My parents' marriage was under considerable strain largely because my father, strong willed and determined to have his way at all odds had taken another wife. Her name was Comfort. In days of old it was not unknown for a woman to "marry a wife" for her husband especially in instances where the man was impotent or the wife was barren and could not bear children. This however was not the case in our household. Father wanted another wife, as was the practice to show that he had taken his rightful place in the community and perhaps subconsciously to fill the vast void left by the death of my sister, Obiageli who died of complications from measles in 1956, before my birth in 1959 at Kaduna Military Hospital in Kakuri in northern Nigeria. Unbeknownst to my mother, while they were living in Enugu, traditional nuptial formalities had been concluded in Onitsha. Comfort, the new wife remained at my uncle Ofili's house in Onitsha until my father was ready for her to meet my mother. From all accounts it was a frosty evening for all concerned. Both women were soon disillusioned with the arrangement and Comfort, young and perhaps a little naive pondered whether being a second wife was what she wanted. Although father appeared to have infinite possibilities and opportunities ahead, she would always be number two wife.

Mother must have been relieved when we moved from the confined quarters of Airways House, which for a time also housed Comfort, wife number two, before her departure for London. Lagos at that time had a lively nightlife dominated by highlife great Bobby Benson's nightclub and the legendary boxing exploits of undisputed world middleweight two-time champion Dick Tiger who was constantly compared to Hogan Kid Bassey another Nigerian boxing great of similar vintage. Among my favorite early memories of Lagos was driving with my father to Bar Beach, as well as Takawa Bay, the city's best known beach, in the late afternoon after a typical tropical flash thunderstorm which saw sheets of rain falling for a few minutes before giving way to cloudless sun filled blue skies. You could smell the rain coming and the cool tropical breeze that announced the thunderstorm. The impromptu outing was a treat after some upsetting mishap at home which caused me to cry. I was very frustrated as a child and found few productive outlets for my intellectual and emotional energies other than the occasional altercation. Looking back and with the experience of having my own gifted children I now realize that my environment and circumstance did not offer the intellectual and physical nourishment I desperately craved but had no basis to articulate. We had few books in the house and no organized activities like music lessons or museums to attend. I certainly remember being bored with play with my peers very

Early Years

early on in my life and grasping crudely for ways to expand my horizon. At the same time, I longed for the emotional connection with my parents that I saw in my elder sister and brother which was impossible then because of the complexities and tragedies in the making playing out in my parent's lives.

As we drove, father comforted me. "Ozugo, kwsi-ibe akwa" (that's enough, stop crying), he said to me in Ibo. He wiped the tears from my eyes with the palm of his hand the way African mothers do. "Kemaka ice-cream?" (How about some ice-cream?), he said, knowing this would bring an instant smile to my face. My tears soon vanished. Lagos traffic and pollution that we know now was virtually nonexistent then and the drive to the beach was serene. The beach had banks of golden sand, tall palm trees and the occasional colonial, part of the imperial hierarchy, shaded under a coconut tree with a Chapman cocktail in-hand enjoying the many bountiful fruits that mother Africa had to offer; ex Africa semper aliquid novi, (Africa always brings something new). I loved the sound of the waves rushing onto the beach and seeing the tall blue-black Hausa vendors in their colorful robes selling delicious suyer (beef grilled on open fires with scrumptious Hausa herbs and spices served on newspapers and garnished with diced onions) along the beachfront. Vendors on bicycles with coolers attached to the front hawked Walls vanilla ice cream, the only flavor we knew, up and down the beach. Vanilla was my father's favorite ice cream. This was one of those very rare occasions that every young boy understands, when I had my father to myself.

Life for me revolved around plotting mischievous adventures with Bolaji and our gang, which included the aptly named Pa-Po-Pa-Po who had a huge belly button like an old fashion squeezable car horn. We wheeled bicycle rims with metal coat hangers energetically through the streets and plucked exotic fruit: papaya, mango, and udala, when in season with long sticks. Sometimes we accidentally disturbed lizards and dozing snakes curled high on the upper limbs of fruit trees and swiftly retreated in fright blissfully unaware of the life threatening dangers we were imposing on ourselves. We made trumpets from the limbs of papaya trees, saved garri (local staple: ground and dried cassava eaten with a variety of delicious soups; also very good for use as gum paste for making paper kites), newspapers, and thread from my mum's Singer sewing machine for our homemade kites. We chewed and sucked freshly machete cut sugar cane, watched men nimbly strap themselves to palm trees to shin to the top to tap sap from the trees to ferment to make emu (palm wine), a milky deliciously refreshing and potent local brew which had many a man a-cropper, three sheets to the wind, drunk, banished to slumber under the stars by "her indoors". We bought deliciously smelling six inch yellow penny loaves of bread after church on Sundays which countered the ghastly smell of cheap melting rubber flip-flop slippers on pavements en route home on intensely hot days. Those who had neither slippers nor Bata sandals (Czech cobbler Tomas Bat'a founded Bata in 1894, he was the Henry Ford of shoes, and the company was the largest manufacturer of shoes for the developing world) stayed indoors for fear of burning their feet. We watched and listened to traditional wandering Yoruba drummers, bards with talking drums firmly clasped under their armpits beating rhythmically from street-to-street, and paused to view the spectacle of apprehended burglars quivering, and naked being rubbed down with red-hot chili peppers as punishment after a thrashing with Kobokos (whips) in the burning afternoon sun. This, I might add, cured even the most ardent neighborhood burglar. There were no secrets on Shackleford Street. We watched and jeered the coming-and-going of night-soil workers. These latrine men collected and carried human waste, excreta, in buckets on their heads in the evenings from nearby homes that did not have running water. Equally curious were the mysterious men who appeared from time-to-time, as if from space, with tanks strapped to their backs and Wellington boots, spraying stagnant pools of water in the surrounding lagoons to protect against mosquitoes. We tormented the poor man who lived in the ruins of an old English fort with taunts and insulting chants of "Ole, Ole, ..." (thief) in Yoruba, which one hot still afternoon drove him to appear enraged through the haze firearm in hand, bloodshot eyes wide-open he shouted in Yoruba: "I will dispatch instant justice upon any child foolhardy enough to utter "thief" in my presence". We participated in dangerous games, where we dared each other to jump from the second floor of buildings under construction into the sand below. One day my younger brother Nonso (Martin) missed the target and broke his leg; there was hell to pay when my mum arrived. Wounds and scratches were treated with local plants we plucked from the bush around us. These native remedies were remarkably effective at relieving itches, quickly staunching bleeding, and healing wounds and many other tropical aliments. The onset of urban sprawl made these plants harder-and-harder to find in the city. If only I could remember what the plants were today, I'd be a rich man. We were "City boys" cut-off from the close-knit village roots that our parents had known. I walked to school for afternoon lessons in the burning sun clad in my uniform: green shorts and white shirt; St. Paul's in Ebute Metta was my first school with its rows of wooden benches and no glass louver panes in the windows to shelter us in the rainy season. The open window frames served to keep us cool in the blistering hot summer. We made deliciously refreshing "organic" drinks with my siblings from honeysuckle blossoms and water, sweetened with a teaspoon of sugar. Nectar gave the blossoms a sweet aromatic scent. We caught and caged crickets in the long grass, some green and some various shades of brown, as well as beautiful bright yellow canaries. On the way home from school, despite stern warnings from our parents, we sometimes scavenged through putrid waste in the local dump like Slum Dog Millionaires searching for buried treasure. Our play was usually outside in the open air and was almost always full of imagination and inventiveness. We were blissfully unaware of the seamy side of existence and the deprivation and the dramas of the world beyond our neighborhood.

Bolaji and I were in constant search of adventure, one day we spotted a new car parked outside a neighbor's house. This was unusual since cars were still relatively rare in the neighborhood and paved roads were few-and-far between. For some inexplicable reason we decided to throw stones at each other over the sparkling new car. Our enthusiasm soon got the better of us and we were throwing stones with reckless abandon and laughing wildly. It was only a matter of time before a stone breached the windscreen with the voluble crash of breaking glass. The rotund owner dashed out wailing and looking as if he had lost a child. He chased us down the street screaming and cursing. Soon police arrived and my weeping mother placed a woman's head-scarf over my head to protect me from the lice I would likely encounter in the cells of the local rat infested constabulary. Meanwhile the Black Maria idled impatiently waiting for its young passengers. Fortunately the neighbors were able to console the car owner in his grief with a promise from our parents to pay for repairs. This spared us both from incarceration at the tender age of six but did little to halt the thrashing from our mothers that awaited us once inside. Our neighbors in the meantime delighted themselves debating with the policemen and women whether it was Lanre No.: 1 or Lanre No.: 2 who threw the errant stone. Lanre was a common local name like "Joe" or "John" which our neighbors used to refer to Bolaji and me. This encounter however did not dampen my enthusiasm for wandering the neighborhood with Bolaji and playing football way beyond the time allotted by my mother, which meant sneaking in through the ground floor window and tiptoeing to my room. My mother cleverly waited for me to settle-in; with me believing I had outwitted her before pouncing to meter out her customary unzobu unzobu punishment.

During this period, I also have memories of my very beautiful cousin Theresa and her brother Okey, who lived with us in Lagos until the terrible tragedies that precipitated the Nigerian civil war and led to the family settling in London. Theresa later eloped with her lover Sonny, bore a son and settled next door in disgrace, shunned in exile from our family. We were forbidden to see her. My father likely felt that we had let down Theresa and her family in our duties as her ward. This harsh punishment that my mother dutifully followed, I am sure against her better judgment, did not stop us from periodically sneaking in to see Theresa and her beautiful son, although there would be hell to pay if we were caught as occurred on occasion. Their cramped dimly lit home was located off a long corridor you entered from the street through a ragged coarse dark-blue cotton curtain. It was equipped with the ubiquitous trappings of urban Lagos existence: a ceiling fan, dual burner Calor gas cooking stove, and Vono enameled metal bed with a thin two inch mattress on stretched springs. A colorful ute (raffia sleeping mat) rolled-out on the gloss painted concrete floor lay next to the bed. The baby was usually the first to receive visitors crawling to the doorway with a gigantic contented smile. A Spartan abode drenched, like Romeo and Juliet, with the infectious carefree glow and laughter of a young rebellious couple deeply in-love.

This subterfuge continued until Theresa tragically vanished, presumed killed perhaps because of her beauty in the rush to flee what presaged the brutal pogroms against western educated and prosperous commercial minded Ibos who dominated trade in most parts of the country. The pogroms and other troubling events rocked Nigeria and sent the country into a bloody and brutal two-and-half year civil war. Theresa's death was very painful and hard to comprehend for a six year-old. She was a big sister to us all. The family struggled to cope with creeping civil strife -- rumors of coups and counter-coups that engulfed and eventually descended into full-blown civil war only seven years after the exuberance of Independence in 1960. The civil war dashed the hopes and lives of many bright and able young men who found themselves on the wrong side of the war, cutting short whatever aspirations they had of leading Nigeria to its new position in the modern world. For me a six year-old it was terrifying knowing sudden death could come to me and my family at any moment as had been

Early Years

the case for my cousin Theresa. Our home was no longer a safe sanctuary.

Back in Lagos again secreted among our remaining loyal neighbors, one of the very talkative secretaries in my father's office, who lived close by, tipped-off my mother about the impending danger that lingered as tensions mounted in the north of the country ahead of the pogroms that were to follow that September of 1966. Mother took-off the distinctive patterned wrapper and headscarf that marked her as Ibo. Disguised in unaccustomed traditional Yoruba garb, Buba (dress), with an Iro (wrapper) over her left shoulder and Gele (headscarf), my mother went immediately to see Alhaji Sanusi a senior official at the Nigeria Airways office in Ikeja, Lagos who was on his way to a meeting outside the office and directed one of his subordinates to contact my father to authorize tickets for our travel. That subordinate was subsequently killed in the massacre of Ibos. Fearing the worst, in late-August 1966, my father arranged tickets for us to travel to London a step ahead of the bloody pogroms; the thought was that we would all return home to Nigeria with my mother once things were calmer. This would be the subject of heated debate in the weeks ahead between father, mother and separately, Comfort. Father was in a unique situation to follow unfolding developments at home having access to daily travelers with news from all parts of the country and through the national network of offices that coincidentally arranged travel logistics for ranking military personnel, their heightened travel activity itself being a red flag for pending hostilities.

The scene at Ikeja airport was chaotic and fraught with fear and tension. The fragrance of kerosene filled the air. I gazed as well placed Ibos with means fled en masse by air, sea, and land, watched resentfully by Federal troops and officials from the North and southwest, some of whom would soon join the killing frenzy of the September pogroms. I was terrified. I cried uncontrollably through the frightening ordeal. I cannot remember all the details surrounding our departure, but going to the airport it was not clear by any means that my brave desperate mother would board our flight alive with my four siblings, two older and two younger, and me, or whether death awaited all of us at the airport.

I do however recall the equal sense of panic at the inoculation center where my mother had taken us some days earlier before we received our passports and tickets that would see us free from the pending hell in Nigeria. My mother was stressed and frightened; people around us were screaming angrily pushing eager to be processed to escape. I feared being trampled by the army of fleeing Ibos and had a keen sense of impending danger even if I did not fully understand why and what had gone array in the body politic of Nigeria. I understood the imperative of getting on the flight and out of Nigeria preferably alive. I hoped and prayed that I was born lucky.

Some days earlier a group of terrified mothers appeared unexpectedly at my school weeping and breathlessly wailing having run non-stop from the busy and popular Ido bus-stop and motor-park where false rumors had spread among Ibo and Yoruba traders that soldiers were approaching from Ido Bridge. This triggered a mass stampede in which my mother was caught-up. She was fortunate not to have been trampled in the panic that ensued. Stalls where overturned; and she was among the mothers at the school gate having run non-stop from the motor-park stopping only at the British West African Bank to withdraw all the money in her account there. At the bank, fraught depositors jostled each other in disorderly lines to withdraw their meager savings. Weeping mothers hastily collected their children from class in panic and scattered, hearts still pounding, to the presumed safety of their distant homes. Breathless, on the way home, my elder brother Regi announced, "Mummy, mummy, many soldiers in uniform came with big guns. They landed on the school sports field. There was dust everywhere from the loud swirling blades of the camouflage painted helicopters!"

3. London

Safely on board after passing through a terrifying gauntlet of officials we breathed a huge sigh of relief. The sight of the plane door being closed by a male steward comforted us. The Vickers VC10 aircraft taxied and took-off bound for London. We looked out of the windows at a sprawling chaotic airport down below. It was my first experience flying and I remember the calming presence of the glamorous British Overseas Airways Corporation (BOAC) airhostesses and being taken with my siblings to have our "Jet-Club" books signed and mileage recorded manually by the pilot. (Imagine doing that today each time you want to log air miles). The food was inedible but the excitement and palpable relief made me forget my hunger. The safe and secure environ of the air-conditioned fuselage contrasted vividly with the overpowering heat at the airport, buzzing mosquitoes, bluebottle flies, the smell of disinfectant, and the probable death we narrowly escaped.

It was with some considerable relief that we landed at a cold and damp Queen's Terminal at London Heathrow. The unpleasant and unaccustomed climate was a major shock to my system. I had never seen so many white faces. We descended the stairs from the aircraft and were met on the tarmac by my father and chauffeur who ushered us into the cavernous bowels of a majestic jet-black Daimler limousine for the drive to Golders Green in North West London. In those days passport formalities were expedited for VIPs and our luggage would be collected and delivered in another limousine along with our passports which had the prized "Entry Certificate" stamp which gave "leave to enter the United Kingdom for an indefinite period", conferring permanent residency similar to a U.S. Green Card.

There was clearly tension in the air from the moment of our arrival and apprehension as to what awaited us in what was, after all, Comfort's home. The house was not as I imagined, in fact it was what they called a flat, which clearly had not been built to accommodate seven rambunctious children and two wives. For the next couple of months we managed as best we could and grew accustomed to the frequent bickering between the two wives which revolved around which plates should be used, which children should bathe when and who should share Mr. Udo's bed. It was apparent that multiple wives were harder to manage in the suburban confines of London.

Comfort, the mild mannered second wife, a teacher by profession was from the well-known Adibua family of respected lawyers. She was a tall statuesque woman with pleasant engaging features; they had two children, Lauretta and Sammy, my half-brother and sister who settled in a comfortable company flat in Golders Green. The back of the flat overlooked our landlady's garden with its enticing red apples that we lusted after but could not gain access to. Directly at the other end of the garden, were open French doors of a synagogue where bemused we watched worshipers rocking back and forth, in Shabbat service on Friday evenings. Golders Green was popular among newly arrived African diplomats. Tolerant Jewish intellectuals who gladly welcomed fellow upwardly mobile respectable rent paying emigrants to the neighborhood had long settled this leafy suburb. It was from here that my father would be chauffeured in his jet-black company Vanden Plas Princess with walnut trim and folding tables, and fine leather upholstery, by his uniformed, capped and gloved

OYIBOS

English chauffeur to his office on New Bond Street in central London.

New arrivals like my father were not insensitive to the up-lifting virtues of reverse colonialism. Father's shirts, remarkably in a nation not famed for service until recent decades, were laundered and delivered to our doorstep, crisp and suitably starched by an outside service, Advance Laundry, in rectangular boxes neatly folded in paper bags with see through cellophane fronts. Although we lived fairly comfortably in Nigeria, I was amazed by all the modern conveniences of life in London. Father flew to the Mercedes Benz factory in Stuttgart, West Germany to acquire a dark blue Mercedes Benz 220 SE with full specs, which included a newly introduced built-in Philips compact record player. He drove the car back to London from Stuttgart for private use to the many weekend functions that his work and station demanded. Not long after my father's proud acquisition, he was involved in a crash in the Heathrow Airport tunnel, which put the Benz out of commission for some weeks while it was repaired and restored to shinning glory. This was not his first accident, he had almost died in a horrendous car crash in Nigeria before my birth when his speeding car spun-off the road and tumbled into the bush. The car was wrecked but Mr. Udo emerged miraculously from the boot (trunk) with only a dislocated thumb and some scratches and bruises.

Dressed in black-tie or alternatively for more casual occasions, in stylish brown suede desert boots and drain-pipe trousers, cardigan and a silk cravat, Roxy with Comfort were part of fashionable London in the Go-Go sixties. This included Garden parties at Buckingham Palace for the newly minted Commonwealth diplomatic enclave in London. Here new arrivals would sip tea and eat cucumber sandwiches with the Queen and other distinguished guests and discuss among other things schooling and boarding schools for their offspring. "Eton or Harrow, which one do you prefer?" Eton was out of favor following the controversial book Nigger at Eton, by Dillibe Onyeama who was among the first African students at Eton. His great-grandfather was a fearsome Ibo king and was rumored (unconfirmed and challenged) to have buried one of his unfaithful wives alive. Onyeama operated an intricate and highly efficient network of secret police in his domain that gathered information and reported on its citizens. Tipped-off that he may be arrested; he met with an untimely death. Apparently as a result of suicide from self-inflicted gunshot wounds on his way by train to make peace with the white colonial rulers after many years of resisting British rule. Their family attended the same church as we did, St. Edward the Confessor, in Temple Fortune where the aged cleric Father De Fillies presided over weekly mass and ministered his flock. Through a quirk of fate I was to later meet Dillibe's brother and sister in Geneva, Switzerland. The former being a good friend and past work colleague of my college roommate, he is now the number two, Assistant Director-General at the World Intellectual Property Organization (WIPO), a victory of sorts for his great-grandfather perhaps.

Father and Comfort moved easily between this and the small elite community of West Africans in London. Meanwhile my father had to navigate the dichotomy of his sophisticated Western life style with the demands of the village community back in Onitsha. He also had to contend with the anomaly of two wives in her majesty's realm. The joyful glow of tight knit village life still burned in him although he was thousands of miles away. He was an active patron of the Onitsha Union of the United Kingdom and Northern Ireland, which he chaired for a period, traveling the length and breadth of the country championing the virtues of Onitsha culture and custom. We missed his absence at home and longed to play seesaw on his legs and feet. Sometimes his duties took him to the less salubrious corners of England where the occasional Onitsha family through misfortune had been forced to locate, usually because the father, forlorn, homesick, and disillusioned with inequities in England had abandoned his post or studies. My father mediated family disputes, separations, frowned upon divorces and unions with the British, and made speeches at weddings and Christenings.

Roxy's prized Benz was in much demand for the weddings of favored friends and distant relatives in London. Suitably decked in pink or white ribbons it would ferry the bride and groom to the church in style where car and occupants would be showered with confetti after the ceremony by waiting guests. Guests, were elegant in their sixties fashions and women dressed-to-kill in their beautiful brightly colored appliqué George wrappers and prints made from four yards of cloth, elaborate headscarves and gold jewelry. Body painting with indigo dye or camwood, which was the hallmark of a single woman in bygone days, however was not evident. Children mingled among the crowd busily eating the many delicious offerings and dancing to both traditional highlife and Ibo numbers and Motown hits. Older children strained to hear idle village gossip, adult tongues loosened with alcohol, usually concerning the various guests and their romantic or professional entanglements while wives vented and struggled to discipline spouses with wandering lusting hands and eyes. It was rare to leave such occasions without some pronounced incident to feed the community's lust for gossip until the next gathering typically at the monthly Onitsha Union meeting.

Father once returned with the sad, gruesome and disturbing tale, which I innocently overheard, of a mother in deep postnatal depression who attacked her unsuspecting husband with a meat cleaver. Probably not the kiss or embrace the husband was expecting to receive after a hard day's labor. He was maimed but survived, and one suspects his ardor may have been cooled, at least for some time thereafter. Father's brief was to generally ensure the wellbeing of the local Onitsha community. This he did with singular devotion while also tending the travel needs of senior State officials and their families, students, traders and other business travelers plying back-and-forth between London and Nigeria. Tourists were far-and-few between save for the odd eccentric Westerner eager for a taste of the Dark Continent. It was a curious job, technical and financial in some facets but also social. Duties on-the-one extreme included arranging for the mortal remains of Nigerians unfortunate enough to perish in the Queen's realm to be shipped home, and on-the-other attending Farnborough Air Show. He provided input on selection of planes for the airline fleet, and as he related in New York some months before his unexpected death, was required to be sensitive to the curious sexual proclivities of certain visiting dynastic dignitaries. He participated in the organization of the "winds of change" visit of the Tory UK Prime Minister Harold Macmillan and Ted Heath to Nigeria in January 1960, ahead of independence in October of the same year. He also made time to visit with and socialize with colleagues and subordinates, particularly attractive female ones. Women were attracted to my father in a way that is hard to describe other than as magnetic and almost hypnotic, a burden alas I have not been blessed with.

My father's cozy arrangement of an independent London and Lagos household was soon to be irreparably shattered. In the meantime I busied myself becoming familiar with eating cornflakes for breakfast rather than the hearty bowl of plantains, yams, and delicious chicken stew to which I was accustomed. Keen to adapt, I tried Tizer, Bovril, Marmite soldiers, and acquired a strong taste for Horlicks malted milk tablets. I marveled at the gold, silver and red top milk bottles that were magically delivered daily to our doorstep with no cows in sight. I also worked on my rudimentary English in front of the television and was stunned to discover that the so called natives in Tarzan were speaking prosaic Yoruba lines like: "you lift me up you put me down" interspersed with Swahili. How could civilized self-respecting subjects of Her Majesty the Queen be taken in by this patently obvious deception? Don't any of them have even a modicum of understanding for African geography and language?

Comfort was a big television fan, as were most Londoners of that era. Through her viewing habits I was introduced to British classics like, All our Yesterdays (a great yawn, featuring Second World War footage and commentary), Captain Scarlet and the Mysterons (my undeniable favorite), Coronation Street, this was Comforts favorite, Doctor in the House a humorously conceived plot set in a hospital, Never Mind the Quality Feel the Width (a genius comedy with Milo O'Shea which deserved prizes based on the name alone), and of course University Challenge with Bamber Gascoigne, "your starter for two". Bamber should not be confused with the professional footballer Gaza of more recent vintage with the same surname who is as famous off the pitch as he was on having been sectioned for a brief and unfortunate period under the U.K.'s Mental Health Act.

I found other distractions, like football in Basing Hill Park, where I would head with my new friends on the few days it did not rain. Corrugated air raid shelters buried underneath what should have been pristine and perfectly flat football pitches disturbed the level topography of the park. The sod on the pitches served as aerial camouflage. The undulations created by the subterranean air raid shelters moderated the skill level in our game and ensured that England's 1966 World Cup victory would not be repeated any time soon. One wondered how they could have provided adequate shelter from Hitler's bombs so close to the surface. London's parks, like its museums, were a repository of the country's war years and the terror wrought by Hitler's V-1 flying bombs, colloquially known as doodlebugs. The not so distant memory of Briton's own recent history of war would also serve later to engender deep seated sympathy among its populace for the Biafran cause, although not deep enough to stop the government from siding firmly with the might of the Federal forces and its economic interests. As the weeks passed by I decided I rather enjoyed living in London. I was sharing bunk beds in the dining room with my immediately younger brother, Nonso, with whom, not surprisingly; I had a somewhat prickly relationship. Nonso had recurring nightmares brought on I suspected by all our family stresses. "Mummy, mummy, the elephants, the elephants are trampling me", he would scream at night, mother's presence followed to comfort him: "Ozugo ibe ze na" (it's okay don't cry). When it was time to return to Nigeria I steadfastly refused to go and told my father, "I want to stay with you", which he duly consented to. I am sure this upset my mother and siblings but my mind was made up. It also added to the unfortunate impression that I was a spoiled brat. The truth, from my six year-old perspective, was if I did not stay then all would be lost for my mother, brothers and sisters since my father would be free to abandon us. It was with guilt and sadness that I saw them go.

I paid the price for my plucky heroics, my days were spent as a houseboy, which my mother had feared, running errands back-and-forth to the local shops for Comfort who since giving birth to my cuddly and slightly chubby brother Samuel had increased vastly in girth and seemed little disposed to venture the few blocks to the high road shops with two infants. I normally raced to and from Sainsbury's to keep warm since my thin Anorak seemed hardly adequate for the cold English summer. Mercifully my father had provided a hooded duffle coat with toggle fastening for the pending winter gloom. The result of my haste was that I usually returned with mostly broken eggs from my errands. This did not amuse Comfort. Exasperated, she looked down at me, shook her head and exclaimed, "Azubike Udo!" I am sure she complained to my father. He seemed happy to have at least one of his other children around, but was not aware that I was quietly, intentionally or unintentionally, being punished for staying behind and spoiling a return to harmonious marital bliss in Mr. Udo and wife number two's household.

Various family friends came to visit from time-to-time which raised the household tempo perceptibly. Formalities commenced with the host, my father, presenting, then breaking, and sharing Oji (kola-nuts), a mild stimulant, in accordance with traditional rites among the males in attendance, and then calling his wives to partake. Blessings to the gods accompanied the breaking of the Oji into fragments with a blunt knife. This ritual is the highest symbol of Ibo welcome and hospitality. Bitter tasting kola-nut pieces were passed around, starting and returning to the host on a plate by the youngest able person in the room, which was usually me, to all attending guests who took a piece with their left (dirty) hand respectfully placed under the plate and their right to take a piece of kola-nut. The server, me, taking the last piece in the same manner, concluded this ceremonial ritual. Depending on the occasion, libations might also be given to the gods in thanks for the bountiful blessings that were to come. Despite being raised Catholic traditional beliefs were frequently maintained in parallel with those of Christian and Muslim practice. Some Onitsha people deeming neither incongruous with the other and hence my father having two wives (three in total but only two concurrently) and still taking communion! A bottle of gin would be opened and drops ceremoniously poured on the earth or carpet to appease the deities.

Guests reminisced about Nigeria and caught up on village gossip about the Obi of Onitsha (King), imobi (his Palace or Court), the Annual Yam Festival as well as Ofala Festival which honors the spiritual rededication of the Obi and the impressive athletic and colorful dance masquerades. Regulars included the aging Guinness drinking George (Ojeh) and his young vivacious and pretty wife, Njideka. This was clearly an arranged marriage. Her youthful vigor was incongruous with his balding monk like cranium. Looking back, sexual congress one would guess was lacking in the relationship. Other guests included the Onuma brothers, one a law scholar who I would see years later at my father's burial ceremonies in Onitsha, our kindly Albino relative, the two brothers from our village Alex and Martin, the versatile, enigmatic, and ever entertaining Mr. Effiong, and the Dafes, a tragic family whose story was repeated among too many ambitious immigrant families, sent for a variety of reasons to post-colonial England. Mr. Dafe was a colleague of my father, his two bright and articulate sons tragically perished in their bed-sits from over indulgence; we suspected in illicit drugs unable to either bridge or satisfy the conflicting cultural demands of two very different worlds. Occasionally there would be Chu, a handsome young man who was studying in West Germany and spoke fluent German. He was usually accompanied by stunning Bavarian blonds. I had not yet grown accustomed to discerning white adult faces, so I was not quite sure if it was the same young woman on each occasion, but I concluded that he must have a harem, I'd heard about those among northern Muslims. In any event, I never learned what he was actually studying. The guests would leave late well fed with jollof rice, moyin moyin, chin chin, and other Nigeria favorites, prepared by my mother and Comfort, and fueled with kola nuts, Guinness and "hot drinks": gin, Johnny Walker Black, and brandy. Nigeria is one of the largest consumers of Guinness, introduced by missionaries, in the world. We were under strict instructions not to eat any food prepared by Comfort for fear that wife number two might poison us. Such fears, although unfounded in our case, were not unusual among wives in a polygamous household. Each wife eagerly guarded her nest. The hottest highlife hits from "Cardinal" Rex Lawson and Sir Victor Uwaifo blared from the walnut veneer cabinet of the Grundig Radiogram, interspersed with Jim Reeves, Otis Redding, and Marvin Gaye. I can still see each glistening disk sequentially stacked on the chrome spindle at the center of the spinning turntable. As the night wore on, LPs dropped down one-by-one. We watched as the arm clicked back and then down as the stylus glided effortlessly, occasionally skipping over the vinyl grooves, from circumference to center teasing sound along the way through reverberating stereo speakers. For his hospitality, my father was usually rewarded with prodigious phone bills since the guests took the opportunity to avail themselves amply of our telephone to call around the globe. This led to my father's subsequent habit of padlocking the dial on the telephone when guests were expected. The sight of the padlocked dial was usually a good conversation opener or closer as the case may be as guests wondered how to solve the Rubik's like conundrum of persuading my father to unlock the telephone to reach the soothing voice of the English operator eagerly waiting to politely route their trunk calls around the world.

4. Wessex Gardens

Soon the time came for me to start my English education at Wessex Gardens Primary School. I was excited at the prospect of attending school in England. Many of my classmates like Daniel, one of my first friends at school, were Eastern European Jews. There were also, from what I could discern, a few native born English children like my friend Clifford who lived around the corner from us. His father was an amateur cricketer which I found difficult to get my head around, he was usually absent on the odd Saturday that I was allowed to visit by my parents, presumably playing at Edgebaston, The Oval, or Lords. Cricket player was not a profession that featured among the doctors, lawyers and civil servants of our circle. Clifford's family provided my first exposure to English family life. He was a single child, which was almost unheard of in Nigeria. His mother was wonderfully nice in a way that over-burdened West African mothers in those days typically could not afford to be. She took us by tube (subway) to Saturday cartoon matinees at the local Gaumont cinema in nearby Hendon where we watched two features for £0 0s 6d. Sixpence that's probably less than a dollar in today's money! The prolific value of the British pound reflected imperial vestiges of might. Coins and notes came in a variety of shapes, sizes, and colors, with magical befuddling names: guineas, crowns, florins, half-crowns, ten-bob notes, two-bob bits, pounds (L or £), shillings, sixpence (6d) or a tanner, thruppence (3d), pence (1ds), and half-pence (1/2d).

School seemed very strange; the teachers were relics of a bygone age, of solid World War II vintage, men sporting RAF handlebar mustaches and women, like the elderly but kind, Mrs. Black, who wore charming Victorian cameo brooches and taught elocution lessons to new immigrants like me so we would not embarrass the local populace with our broken English and murderous diction. English is not my native tongue or first language. I can still visualize Mrs. Black urging our class of newcomers to stick our tongues out to annunciate "three" so that our clumsy pronunciation would not be mistaken for the word "tree". Her training would serve me well. I earned many compliments on my accent over the years especially after graduate school when I showed up to interviews and witnessed the visible surprise on the faces of my prospective employer(s) who clearly were expecting a "local lad" (white face) and had forgotten to ask about the provenance of my surname on the phone. Some condescendingly used the coded phrase "Your English is very good". Their tongue in-cheek observations took little account for the fact that I was obliged, as made clear by Mrs. Black from the outset, to master English to survive and prosper in England, a country that seemed ambivalent for me to become a part of it.

So it was, we took country dancing most mornings in suburban Golders Green, swam in the school's frigid unheated indoor swimming pool -- an activity I detested almost as much as country dancing -- read Alice's Adventures in Wonderland out-aloud, ate goulash, cock-a-leaky soup, and vile rhubarb crumble with custard for lunch and of course observed Guy Fawkes's Bonfire Night and uniquely, in deference to our Jewish neighborhood and community, the High Holy Jewish Holidays. I was overwhelmed by all these many cultural differences. We were multicultural in Golders Green even before it became fashionable in the New Millennium. Nevertheless this was a lot to take-in for a new arrival from the tropics; what for the love of God was the logic of plimsole shod boys prancing around Maypoles in a cold gymnasium in NW11 (the postal code for Golders Green in North West London) with girls dressed in neat white starched pinafores? England and the English profoundly bemused me, so I was glad to make friends with a smart bookish boy named Allen. Another pupil, Robert invited me to his birthday party and ironically gave me a copy of Robinson Crusoe, which of course I could neither read nor comprehend although I spoke two languages fluently, Ibo and Yoruba. I was also keen to be friends with Sarah a smart slightly shy but attractive girl. I am ashamed now to say that I pulled her hair on more than one occasion in country dancing class in vain search for her attention. There was another Nigerian boy, Daniel, who also lived around the corner and who I coincidentally met in Nigeria some decades later as a very successful and affable partner at a prestigious Lagos law firm, a long way from the boy who had on occasion bullied and intimidated me with his towering height. Another West African pupil from Ghana was reported drowned after falling overboard under mysterious circumstances while on a school trip that involved travel by boat. The boy in question was tall for his age, so much so that there was some debate about his actual age. He was feared by most pupils and parents alike and was rumored along with an Eastern European boy to be luring and buggering unsuspecting boys in the washrooms. This news naturally was not well received by the parents of boys at the school; the English school system had not yet sufficiently evolved to have adopted social workers and psychologists to help these boys modify their predatory anti-social behavior.

At the end of the school day Ken or Mike the chauffeur picked me up and took me to my father's office where the secretaries gave me wafer thin ham and cheese sandwiches prepared with archetypical British reserve for tea, and McVites Rich Tea chocolate digestive biscuits, which I adored. I also unwittingly became a tea connoisseur having been designated to prepare tea in the style of the British for guests at home. Ken had on at least one occasion blithely travelled to Nigeria with my father as his chauffeur, something that did not go unnoticed among the Lagos elite ever eager to outdo one another. This became known locally as the "My Mercedes is bigger than yours syndrome". My father's arrival with a white chauffeur caused pandemonium. Ken seemed to love all things Nigerian, its women and especially the spicy hot cuisine. I would not have been surprised if Ken was proficient in complicated and oftentimes baffling Ibo idioms. Even after my father had lost his job and was returning to Nigeria to take up a new post. Ken wanted to move to Nigeria to work for him there. Mike on-the-other-hand, although he was from British Guyana, was a typical city wise Londoner. I always wondered how they came to work for Nigeria Airways and the conversations they must have had at home about their daily adventures working for West African gentlemen. Sometimes on the way home, Mike would drop my father off to visit "colleagues" while Mike and I stayed in the car. Father would return visibly energized from his encounter. Despite Mike's nods and winks it was only later, that I realized the clandestine purpose of his Cinq à Sept liaisons. Occasionally, for my patience I was rewarded with sweets (candy, i.e., not pudding) brought to the car by smiling "aunties", a small price to pay for the silence of the innocent. Father's indiscretions were sadly commonplace, like those of Frenchmen of a certain age whose peccadilloes were met with sangfroid by their wives. At my tender age I had no real view on the matter other than it seemed a trifle odd and uncomfortable; this prompted me to wonder if father might take a third or fourth wife in the future.

London in those days was relatively unhurried and the drive from New Bond Street to 4 Woodstock Avenue in Golders Green took about 30 minutes cutting through the West End, Swiss Cottage, sometimes detouring by Little Venice and its delightful canal barges, the leafy Finchley Road or the beautiful tree lined Hampstead Heath. I usually entertained myself watching London's iconic red double-decker Routemaster buses and remarkable black cabs dodging nimbly between what seemed like uniform round shaped black, dark-blue and bottle-green cars. The cars were almost without exception made in Briton, harking back to the glory days of British industry and might. There were Aston Martins, Austin Healeys, Jaguars, Ford Anglia and Consuls, Hillmans, Humbers, MGs, Morris Minors, Singer, Sunbeams and Wosleys, each with its own unique smell determined by the proportion of synthetics and natural materials comprising the interior and all with dodgy heating and ill-fitting windows and windscreen wipers. Curved shaped corrugated Nissen huts, makeshift housing for World War II blitzed residents, punctuated the landscape here-and-there and "lollipop" crossing ladies with beehive hairdos and miniskirts aided school children across the road.

The local populace seemed impervious to the sight of a chauffeured West African gentleman and his son wending their way home in their glistening Vanden Plas Princess sedan, testimony to the remarkable tolerance of the British toward "bloody foreigners", even Wogs (Western Oriental Gentlemen) as we were less politely referred to among uncharitable and ignorant elements of the loutish English underclass and certain xenophobic upper-class pricks. This was juxtaposed by the kindness shown by our Jewish English landlady who endured the noise of stampeding children and quarreling wives from the upstairs flat. It was she who greeted us when we arrived at the Golders Green flat, enquiring who we were and stunned when my mother informed her that she was Mrs. Udo. Our landlady replied that Mrs. Udo was already upstairs, to which my mother replied this is the "real" Mrs. Udo, Mr. Udo's "senior wife," and marched upstairs with children in-tow leaving our bemused landlady behind.

I recall a strange incident, when my father had to go to the airport after work and took me with him. On arrival at the airport we headed to the Terminal but sensing I was tired my father sent me back to the Benz in the car park. Exhausted and longing for the arms of Morpheus I climbed into the first car that looked vaguely like my father's and fell asleep. Two burly English Bobbies who were startled to find a "colored" little boy fast asleep in the back seat of their police car awaked me from my slumber. The panic in their faces subsided when they saw my father approach and enter the car next to theirs. Confusion resolved. On the way home my father laughed and teased me as to how I missed the flashing lights and large silver bells on top of the vehicle and the words "**POLICE**" emblazoned in bold white letters on the side of the car. I struggled to explain that the wits of a sleepy six year-old could not be compared to that of an adult with or without a full quota of sleep. I fell back to sleep to the relaxing melody of heavy rain and The Beach Boy's "Good Vibrations" on the radio as we raced past the huge flashing neon Lucozade advertisement on the newly constructed Heathrow flyover. Till this day that song and the tale of Goldilocks and the Three Bears evoke my encounter with the two kindly and befuddled British Bobbies.

Equally strange was an audition at the BBC for radio and television advertisements for the BBC's foreign broadcasts in the former colonies that my father took me to at the invitation of a friend. Several smiling male and female English faces, a cameraman, and sound technician greeted us at the studio. Through plate glass in front of us, I could see sound tracks being recorded in sealed rooms across the hall. Giggling children were running about in the corridors in an array of costumes to sets to perform for advertisements that were in production. Seated in the studio ill prepared and frightened as to what to expect, I was confronted with challenges reading the difficult script, and my father struggled to comprehend why his brilliant six year-old had not yet conquered English language and culture in his brief two months in the UK. It struck me as a rather harsh reaction but consistent with father's very high standards for his children. We never spoke about the audition again.

Father and I nevertheless were slowly but surely bonding, although on occasion I still chaffed at the very high standards he expected of his six year-old. He proudly pushed me forward in front of visiting friends and colleagues. I admired the ease with which father navigated life among the English and the seemingly high regard with which he was held among our community of West Africans. Father had ease with life outside home and work that was a joy to marvel. He had a facility for connecting with people and an easy way about him that might explain his magnetism where women were concerned. He oozed success and confidence and knew everyone there was to know in our circles in a new and exciting age.

5. Biafra

My mother and siblings had returned to Nigeria in October 1966. But just two months later with civil war looming, my father again arranged for them to return to London in December 1966. Being in London, this time round I did not endure the torture it must have been to escape out of the country amid even worse chaos and just days before civil war hostilities were formally declared. I did however miss the company of my siblings and my mother, particularly since Lauretta and Sammy were very young to actively play with. It was a relief and joy to have my Lagos siblings safely back in London. It was thanks to my kindly uncle Simon who again interceded with my father, and the courage of my mother, that they were snatched from the likely prospect of death in the violence that erupted in January 1967. The war saw desperate consequences for millions of Biafrans who died of starvation in eastern Nigeria as a result of food and medicine blockades by the Federal forces assisted with arms by various governments including the United Kingdom. Like Iraq today, the politics of oil was a major feature of the Biafran civil strife.

Each evening transfixed we watched the six o'clock BBC news on television, following the unfolding tragedy that was the Biafra conflict and worrying about loved ones back in Onitsha and Lagos. "Look at those poor children", my mother would say, as we watched frightening newsreel images of the genocide. The black and white newsreels showed emaciated Biafran children with Kwashiorkor. Their stomachs and ribs protruding due to an acute lack of protein, which caused thinning hair, premature grayness, arrested growth, weight loss, and other visible signs of advanced malnutrition, and Beriberi triggered by vitamin deficiency. I was haunted by these images. This was the first crisis that was widely covered on television. I can still see these sad and painful images in my mind today. Media spotlight called for an international response which came in the form of humanitarian airlifts dropped by mercenary pilots, the most notable of whom was the eccentric Swedish aristocrat Count Carl Gustav von Rosen, through the makeshift airstrip at Uli. Irish priests, nuns, and French doctors poured into Biafra to help those who were starving or in need of last rites. The French-led aid workers later formed an international medical and humanitarian aid organization Médecins Sans Frontières (Doctors without Borders) to respond to emergency human disasters like Biafra caused by armed struggle.

My father had other headaches too. The government of Her Majesty the Queen had informed him that he in turn must inform the authorities which of his wives was the official wife since the UK did not permit polygamy. My mother as the first wife was given the mantel of official wife. It was not long after that Comfort quietly decamped one day with my brother and sister for sanctuary and peace of mind in her own home while my father was at work. After initial hostilities during which we did not see Lauretta and Sammy, Comfort returned to Nigeria and visited my Father from-time-to-time in his Broad Street office in Lagos and his home in Ebuta-Metta and Yaba to discuss the needs of the children who were subsequently transplanted to live with my father on his return to Nigeria. I've sadly never had an opportunity to discuss with my half-siblings what they made of their sudden return to Nigeria. Meanwhile in London, reunited with my siblings, I imparted my newly acquired knowledge of English etiquette.

"This one they call sandwich after Oyibo man called Earl of Sandwich".

My siblings drew closer around the breakfast table with quizzical interest.

"Two slices of bread with marmalade sauce inside like this."

"You chop (eat) am for breakfast with tea like so".

We waited excitedly for snow, which we had seen in books and television but had not experienced. Our dream came true one winter morning as we made our way to school at Wessex Gardens without boots, hats, or gloves. My father however curiously equipped us with the ubiquitous leather satchel harnessed to our backs that was the signature of London school children of that era. The snowflakes were beautiful beyond my imagination. They looked magical as they tumbled from the dark sky to the white covered pavement (sidewalk). Virgin snow covered the road ahead and the odd footprint could be seen leaving clues who had passed-by, a child, adult, dog or bird. Snowballs whistled past our ears, thrown by other children on the way to school. Some stopped to build snowmen and to tumble in the white powder. They seemed to be having fun. We looked on in wonderment and chatted among ourselves unsure how to react and what to do with snow. This was all new and strange for me and my excitement was tempered by the biting cold wind and the absence of warm comforting layers around my vulnerable beautiful brown form. Worse still, my spare athletic West African frame had negligible body fat to insulate from the unfamiliar discomfort of the cold. After our snowy encounter we had our first run-in with the painful swelling and throbbing of chilblains made worse by warming our hands and toes on the nearest radiators.

OYIBOS

Now ensconced in London and being too young, my brother Regi and I mercifully escaped having to return to Nigeria against imponderable odds with wooden rifles. We were left to wrestle with the task of assimilating in London, and dealing with the shadow of war and the guilt of being among those fortunate enough to have escaped. The futility of war was apparent to me even at this tender age. These experiences and the terrifying book in my father's cabinet, published by the Biafran propaganda machine in London, showing severed heads, mutilated bodies, and other atrocities against Biafrans imbued in me a profound distaste for war and the vile weapons of man's savagery that accompany it. Fittingly our family name, "Udo" means "Peace" in Ibo.

Shortly after Comfort's departure, my father was dismissed from his post after refusing several "promotion" offers to return to Nigeria. He was painfully aware of the fate of other Ibo colleagues who having been lured back were slaughtered right there on the tarmac at Lagos's Ikeja Airport with machetes. My parents had speculated that dismissal would only be a matter of time but nevertheless when it came it was a body blow for my father. Gloom followed for all. The trappings that came with the job were lost one-by-one, the Princess, Daimler limousine, chauffeurs, flat and other privileges. My father kept his beloved Mercedes 220 SE and found a clerical job at Smiths Industries, makers of aircraft instrumentation and watches, a curious and bewildering product combination that was doomed to eventual failure. The only benefit I could discern from his new post was the occasional gift of a mediocre watch that failed to keep accurate time and the cracking children's Christmas party that the firm hosted. His morale was low but there was nothing else to do since prospects of a senior executive position at BEA or BOAC were virtually non-existent for those chaps outside the old school tie network and of a certain complexion. BOAC was the forerunners to British Airways. BEA was the domestic carrier and BOAC was the imperial overseas carrier. One day my father returned home from his work more despondent than usual, when my mother asked where the Mercedes was. He said he had had to sell the car after his union boss saw him opening and entering the car to drive away after work. "Mr. Udo", he muttered resentfully, "I see you are not a hard-and-fast supporter of the working classes and I am sure probably will not be voting Labor". Interestingly, legal residents that are non-citizens can vote in general (National) elections in the U.K. My dad drove the car to the dealership immediately and arrived home in a Ford Zephyr, a proletarian vehicle and the ultimate status symbol for a working class man with a large family. To add to this indignity, we children had to take public transport from now on. I still remember the palpable shock and shame the first time I entered a public bus with my mother.

My mother was forced to seek employment, first at the local police cafeteria, then at a factory where she endured the prejudices that were rampant in British society at that time, before finally going to college in the evenings to attain qualifications as a Confectioner making gourmet wedding cakes. She later found work at a local Clarks Bakery and finally many years on at the cafeteria of the nearby British Cancer Research Institute. This was a long way from her childhood ambitions to become a doctor like her half-brother who qualified in London and her early teaching experience in Rivers State before marrying my father. My mother had not deserved such misfortune since she had long cautioned my father, who lived for the moment, to accept the generous low interest mortgage offered by the Airways to senior executives. Mother had hoped in vain that he would seize the opportunity to acquire a home-away-from-home for the family in the sober environs of Golders Green, Hendon, St. John's Wood or Hampstead. Mother was alive to possibilities in a way that my father either did not recognize or chose to ignore preferring to follow his own unfettered authentic traditionalist path back to the village in Onitsha.

My mother in many ways is both a heroine and a paradox. I had much less sense of my mother's interior life growing up and did not have the opportunity to bond with her the way I had with my father until much later in my teen years. Her bravery and presence of mind ensured that I was spared probable death in Nigeria's civil war.

Mother survived a difficult upbringing with feuding parents, benefited from a privileged adolescence under the roof of her well-off aunt, attended school in an era when few Onitsha parents sent girls to school beyond the age of eleven, and survived fifty-years of a precarious polygamous marriage.

Her progressive thinking father, the son of a wealthy farmer and a member of Ndichie, Ozo "Red Cap Chiefs" who were at the pinnacle of social and political authority in Onitsha, was an esteemed court clerk under British colonial rule. He was stationed in the nearby town of Enugu away from his daughter and other wives and children. Given my own experiences, it must have been difficult for my mother not having her father around. Her mother, Agnes Anwuli (Joy), or "Gold" was from respected local linage. She was called "Gold" on account of her beautiful bearing and striking complexion, which gives cause for pause about the antecedence of some of my maternal forbearers and their early encounters with the white colonials. Anwuli told satirical tales of strange mystical Europeans and their arrival on the banks of the River Niger. Folklore has it that Onitsha town's men and women observed the exotic Europeans, (who often perished prematurely succumbing to tropical diseases), with their strange habits, like walking dogs on leashes and sunbathing, with the same eager curiosity as the colonizers watched them.

Anwuli was my grandfather's third and very pretty youngest wife. They had a stormy relationship. She was one of three surviving daughters from thirteen and a member of the prestigious Odu Women's Society that elevates an Onitsha woman's status considerably. Entrance to the society is gained through social standing and wealth in the community. The beautiful heavy ivory bracelets worn on their arms and feet distinguish these Odu women. My mother like her mother is also a member of the Odu Society. She is the eldest of three sisters and was sent to live with her father's well-to-do sister at the age of eight. My grandmother had other thoughts, but had little choice in the matter under local custom and law in that epoch. This early blunt trauma notwithstanding, my grandfather's sister an astute and prosperous market trader was kind to my mother and it was in her home that mother lived until adolescence; it was she that mother called "Nne" (mother).

In my parent's youth it was highly unusual to invest in the education of girls beyond primary school. This however did not stop umu naanyi (women) from excelling within and without the community through raw intellect and guile; some successfully amassed prodigious fortunes by the standards of the time trading in Onitsha's famed market where legend has it that you can buy anything imaginable including the space shuttle. This and other markets were part of networks of market exchanges extending well beyond the confines of Onitsha. They also exercised considerable power through numerous women's groups and associations, e.g., savings unions, as well as age-grade dance groups with distinctive egwu (songs and dances). To demonstrate the powerful clout of women that nwanyi bu ife (women are of worth), the last Queen of Onitsha, Omu Nwagboka (Onye-isi Ikporo-Onicha) famously in 1886 led a successful all women boycott of household and social duties "to remind the community that no society can function without the duties and tasks performed by its women" (From, Gender Equality in a Dual-Sex System: The Case of Onitsha, by Nkiru Nzegwu). This co-dependency was not lost on the reigning male monarch, Obi (King) Anazonwu with who the Queen, the female monarch, had been in conflict. In this spirit, women in my family are typically independent and strong willed; and not at all reticent about pursuing their own lives and professional careers.

My grandfather took the radical and progressive precaution of sending his daughter to secondary school at Africa College; where tellingly as revealed in an old school photograph, mother was the only female in her class of about twenty. She had a brilliant mathematical mind and regularly bested her male peers at school, who in turn were embarrassed about being beaten by a girl. They tried unsuccessfully to bully her in retaliation for her success as a girl. Her wealthy maternal aunt and her husband wanted to send my mother to England for further studies, but her father refused, so she was compelled to teach and was not afforded the opportunity to advance her studies to

Biafra

university (college). All career hopes vanished once mother married; children were born in quick succession.

PART II: The Green Belt: 1966-1979

6. The Real World

One of the few positive events I remember from this turbulent and uncertain time was my father taking me with him to an Indian restaurant for a meal with an Englishman friend from his Airways days. This was my first ever restaurant meal and my last for some time. I can still taste the pungent spices (tamarind, coriander, cloves, and cardamom), infused in the succulent lamb, chicken, and okra sauces, the delicious hot Nan bread and basmati rice. The meal marked the end of innocence and the closing of a chapter for our old lives. It was the start of fresh excursions that would bring us in collision with the "Real World" with challenges afresh, earthy pleasures, and a new kind of soulful happiness. It was the beginning of the end of innocence for my siblings and me. Now nine, my father announced that we were to be resettled as political refugees. We moved into, a four bedroom semi-detached council house (public housing) in the well-heeled conservative suburban neighborhood of Mill Hill East some miles north of Golders Green -- the "East" was used depending on whom you were speaking too. East was used if you were speaking to a local lout like Froggie whose unfortunate visage bore a more than striking resemblance to a frog and hence his nickname. These louts on occasion blocked my passage, and were always eager for a fight or scrape. If on-the-other-hand it was a damsel from the riding school up the hill near the charming and aptly named Mill Hill Village, the "East" was omitted. A horticultural haven, Mill Hill was home to the stately and lavishly appointed Mill Hill School, the late Sir Denis Thatcher's alma mater.

The house was a generous concession given us by the authorities on account of my father's elevated status, our large family by English standards, the country's humane and generous social system, and our predicament as political refugees. It was perhaps the best that we could have expected under the circumstance. Penniless, our family had lost everything: our home in Onitsha, uncle and cousin, my father's pension and savings in Nigeria (Biafra's currency was debased by the victorious Nigerian military forces after the war which demolished generations of wealth accumulated by Ibos) and our dignity and standing within our community. In short, almost all that defined us as a well to do family of foreign extraction living in London. These profoundly negative experiences were cushioned by the beautiful leafy surroundings of Mill Hill and adjacent Green Belt which was accessible on foot through century's old public paths. These led to idyllic destinations like Totteridge with farms and open countryside where we spent lazy summer days happily blackberry picking and apple scrunching or simply watching cricket on a hot summer's day. Cattle, horses, and sheep grazed in ancient acres dotted with charming cottages and baronial manors. To the consternation of my parents, particularly my father, his eldest son, my brother Regi took up riding with a local horse-loving girl Judy, reigniting father's fears that his children would become lost to the world and ways of the Oyibos.

Our new home was relatively spacious compared to the flat, with a garden in front and back and open fields across the road. The house had four bedrooms, running water and "indoor plumbing" but no central heating save for a coal-fired stove for hot water in the kitchen. Father bought an upright out-of-tune piano for my eldest sister Augusta to continue her lessons although we could no longer afford instruction. He clearly hoped this would fill the void left by her unexpected removal from boarding school.

Our cantankerous neighbors except for the elderly stout Mrs. Harris, who lived next door, were not exactly thrilled at our arrival. The cheerful and normally extremely sober Mrs. Harris returned from OAP (Old Age Pensioner) weekend coach (bus) outings to the bright lights of Blackpool visibly tanked, merry, and leg-less. Her industrious and equally nice divorcee daughter Renee aided her down the garden path we shared. I admired her spirit and ability to let-go and move on, to laugh at life, something that was rare among the war generation. Her son on-the-other-hand seemed trapped in time. Bert continued to wear his grey flannel World War II demob (demobilization) suit, brown sleeveless V-neck pullover, and 1930s trilby hat.

My capacity for a scrappy brawl learnt from Shackleford Street I suspected would be put to good use in this neighborhood. There were many Doc Marten's and suspender wearing skinheads in the vicinity with IQs to match their tiny boot sizes. It was these teenage youths, denizens of low-life London, who welcomed us to the neighborhood by hurling racial epitaphs - "wogs, nig-nogs..." - and bricks through our frosted glass front door. My father was incredulous that Britain's polite youth could perform such a cowardly and despicable act. He consoled himself thinking that perhaps I had made up the story to conceal our own boisterous play. This was one of many frightening and humiliating acts we and countless other immigrant families would have to endure as part of our initiation and subsequent assimilation into the broader English community.

Around this time, when I was eight, my school went on a trip to the Isle of Wight where I had the

The Real World

terrifying experience of being targeted, followed, and constantly verbally and physically menaced with kicks by a group of local skinheads, that is, until we ventured to historic and beautiful Osbourne House in East Cowes. It was one of Queen Victoria's favorite retreats. The skinheads clearly had no taste for their own culture, and I am sure that Queen Victoria would not have been amused by the appalling behavior of these local hooligans. They were finally confronted by one of our fiery diminutive female teachers who sent them packing in short order once and for all. Despite the bravado of their menacing appearance these thugs had little stomach for a fight. They were simply for the most part bored dimwits bent on causing misery for young immigrants like myself while searching desperately for meaning in their otherwise dull lives and addled minds.

Plans for me to attend boarding school in the remote wind swept Isle of Man was shelved much to my relief. My sister Augusta and brother Regi who were settled in boarding school in Ireland were forced to leave friends behind and return to the U.K. We could no longer afford the school fees. This despite the fact that my sister was part of the Saint Mary's Dominican Convent Cabra Dublin Irish step dancing team in the 1969 championships held in Sligo. Regi, my rugby playing brother, a student at Terenure College Dublin, would have to find use for his Irish brogue back home in London. My temporary status as eldest in the house with all its privileges would change. No more bedtime at 8:30 PM instead 8:00 PM. These were no small trifles for a nine year-old.

It was here in Mill Hill that my younger brother Amechi was born. As the baby of the family, he received copious love and attention from us all. He was the first child to whom my parents gave an Ibo first name. Amechi was born premature because of the callous and wicked indifference of a Routemaster bus driver who pulled away from the bus stop before my pregnant mother had fully boarded. She tumbled from the speeding bus and went into labor shortly thereafter. My parents received some token compensation from London Transport but not sufficient to warrant the hours of bleeding suffered by my mother after the birth of my brother. I remember us going to Whittington Hospital with my father to visit my mother and asking the nurse if my mother would be okay. We feared she might have a life threatening illness, but instead, we were calmly told: "you have a baby brother love". I had not understood that my mother was pregnant. Amechi would later lose an eye as a toddler from hemorrhaging caused while at his daycare child minder. I recall his continuous crying that night. He would not stay in bed and was clearly out of sorts. Eyes bloodshot, he was rushed to hospital early the next day when it became apparent that his crying was because he was hurt and suffering in pain. This was yet another family trauma in a series that seemed unending.

London's red double-decker buses would feature in our lives again some years later when my immediately younger brother Martin leapt out of the middle doors of a bus at the stop 50 yards from our house and dashed behind the bus excited about his new football (soccer) boots straight into the path of an oncoming car. He was severely injured with a broken fibula, tibia, and multiple contusions, fractures, and abrasions. I had gotten home early from school and was alone, about to make myself a relaxing cocoa when the doorbell rang and I opened the front door to see a terrified neighbor pale with shock. She plainly thought my brother was dead, he or she, I cannot remember the gender because of the shock and trauma engendered by the news, spoke slowly and deliberately "your brother has been knocked-down", "hurry". I cringed with fear at the sight of my brother's crumpled bloody body on the road, I heard the uncontrollable screams of a hysterical woman in the background and the shaken driver trying to explain what had happened. It was like a very, very bad dream, my heart pounding, feeling totally helpless with no adult at hand and unable to help my brother who reached out for my hand as we entered the ambulance and raced to the hospital. After many blood transfusions, surgical procedures and endless months of painful physical therapy, Martin made a full recovery. The trauma was so profound; I could barely bring myself to visit a hospital again.

The accident with Martin left me deeply scarred in a way I did not understand until very late in my life. There had always been intense sibling rivalry between us, both of us competing for the limited attention of my mother and father at a time we were each seeking to establish our own identities within our family and broader group of sometimes overlapping friends and community. The accident triggered many conflicting emotions of pain, guilt, and regret especially for those moments when we squabbled or bickered over some trifle. Our relationship remains difficult and hard for me even today to fully articulate and has always been made even more difficult by our diverging temperaments. Martin's often brooding and unique self-expressed approach to life countered my independent, confident, take-charge "ENTJ" personality, particularly as an early teenager. ETNJ is one of several personality types identified by famed Swiss psychologist and influential thinker, Carl Gustav Jung. I would grow to abhor confrontation; a trait prevalent in those afflicted with an English upbringing, and a source of misunderstanding with American girlfriends in the years to come. America, I was to learn, unlike England and Nigeria, is a society in which disputes are often solved through active confrontation.

A frequent visitor to our home was uncle Arinze, a kinsman from Onitsha but no relation to the famous Cardinal Arinze, the Church's youngest ever Bishop, who also hails from Onitsha and was one of the favored candidates for Pope, after the death of Pope John Paul II. Uncle Arinze worked for the publishing concern ICP and took it upon himself to visit periodically to enquire about our general well-being and most importantly, our academic progress. An anglophile, he had a keen understanding of the English and their traditions and he encouraged and cajoled us to improve our grades and to think about the many opportunities the world of the Oyibos had to offer. He himself was somewhat of a mystery since we had always assumed he was a bachelor but at his death we learnt that he had been married and had boy twins in England from whom he was estranged. He was a tallish cultured and well-spoken man with a Linton Kwesi Johnson (renowned British-Caribbean poet and musician) beard and hat. He wore a gabardine coat whether summer or winter. His own abode was sparingly furnished and strewn with journals and books in organized chaos some might have described him as a stereotypical eccentric Englishman save that he hailed from Onitsha.

His tale was an instructive one. He remarried a young girl chosen from Onitsha, only to learn that she had made learning the rules of marriage and divorce in England a priority in her assimilation and promptly had him evicted from the house thinking the property would now be hers. She calculated wrong however because although he had lived in the house a long time, it was actually rented and the home he owned was in Brixton, rented out to tenants. This is where he decamped until his death when one of his twins emerged to take over the home only to borrow up to the hilt on the property and tragically end up sleeping under cars to keep warm after his eviction. His own death followed not long after that and many months sleeping rough in the harsh bleak English winter. The whereabouts of Uncle Arinze's other estranged son are unknown.

7. Dollis

It was raining outside and I was standing on the stage in the dimly lit school hall in Assembly with the entire school keenly awaiting my match report from our football (soccer) game the previous day against our archrivals, Annunciation. I began reading in my stilting English, my voice quivered, slowly gathering pace and confidence as I went along. I paused for a moment to describe our winning goal: "a spectacular flying shot from Martin Price, into the top right-hand corner of the goal." "Price's shot sent the net billowing out like a sail in a heavy storm." This met with the approving smiles of our skinny headmaster, Mr. Clayton, and applause from the elated audience of children. As captain of the football team I was responsible for reading team match reports every week in front of the whole school at Assembly. This was a terrifying chore which I grew to enjoy despite the watchful gaze of the slender spectacled Mr. Clayton with his shining bald dome.

We played football matches under the tutelage of Mr. Leigh who claimed to have been a former goalkeeper for The Arsenal. Mr. Leigh for some inexplicable reason put me straight into the team after finding out I had played for Wessex Garden's. The first match was played in frigid temperatures on a snowy day in short-sleeves on a pitch that resembled a cow patch with a bladder ball that wrapped around your head when wet and hurt like the dickens if it hit you in the goolies. I thought I would die from the inclement conditions but somehow survived. Games were usually played in driving rain, in our checkered green and white school colors and white shorts. The rain-soaked leather laced ball provided its own peculiar challenges, saturated and heavy with water if kicked viciously it became a weapon with which to fell opposing players, like skittles in a bowling alley. On such days the game was elevated to battle status, those who survived unscathed and still conscious would emerge from the match initiated into manhood having survived two thirty-five minutes halves of mortal combat. For those brave enough to head, the heavy rain-soaked ball thudded against their skulls jarring their brains, it wrapped around the contour of their forehead like putty leaving imprints of the ball's laces before recoiling in slow motion, like a cartoon, from the dazed player's head. Watching mothers, despite objections from the hapless referee would dash on to the pitch periodically to resuscitate sons laid prone by a powerful shot from an opposing player. Half time provided an opportunity for a wet cold sponge to be applied to bruises and sliced oranges to be quickly consumed before resuming battle.

In 1969, I was ten years old, and my siblings and I had witnessed and experienced the random cruelness of change and misfortune that few adults encounter in a lifetime. The excesses of the sixties were coming to an end and a harsh economic decade was just about to begin in the U.K. Dubbed the" winter of discontent" by Maggie Thatcher. The supposed villains of the plot, deservedly or not, were coal miners who deprived many young students the light we needed to study for our O'levels exams because of power-cuts brought on by strikes. It would also mark the influx of Indian Sub-Continent Asian immigrants expelled from Uganda by strongman Idi Amin Dada Oumee, AKA 'Big Daddy' or 'Conqueror of the British Empire'. Their arrival in a time of economic turmoil and change tested Britain's renown for tolerance.

OYIBOS

I started at a new school with my siblings. Dollis Primary School was a short fifty yards walk from our home. The school had a more homogenous student body than Wessex Gardens, relatively young staff and modern facilities. I picked up on this almost immediately and threw myself into sports and my studies, the latter only after some stern talking to from my father. This new school allowed me to flourish; I became more self-confident and aware particularly as my language skills improved, allowing me to overcome the debilitating inarticulateness that banished me to being an outsider at Wessex Gardens. My first day at Wessex Gardens had been terrifying, particularly since my teachers were largely unintelligible to me. By contrast, my two teachers at Dollis, Miss McGowan, a young attractive long-legged and energetic woman, and Mrs. Collins, a handsome, tough, stout, tanned but charming Cypriot married to an Englishman, recognized the rough diamond that I was. They made me believe in myself academically for the first time and did not poke fun at my broken English, which had thankfully been polished by Mrs. Black at Wessex Gardens.

Over my two years at the school, the two teachers provided the nurturing encouragement to improve my class position from the bottom half to the top half of the class. Not bad considering I could barely read and write when I arrived in the country. I recall Mrs. Collins leaning over me to look at a history homework assignment I actually completed and handed-in on time after a long post-bedtime struggle with my dictionary and help from my father who was quick to seize the opportunity to finally pry open his prized Britannica Encyclopedia.

"This is why I bought these [very expensive] books for you children to learn."

Dollis

He cajoled and prodded me as I struggled with the words on the page reading each word out aloud: "The Normans invaded England in..." Father asked the meaning of each long word, and explained those I did not understand the meaning of. He made me memorize each, and I earned a curt wallop on the head for those that I forgot. I cried as I wrote my report but also felt pride and joy for the first time being able to arrange English words and sentences on paper in a succinct way. My teacher Mrs. Collins was amazed.

"Augustine this is fantastic, did you do this by yourself?"

"Well done, I knew you could do it if you tried."

"I expect all your homework to be excellent like this." The exhilarating impulse to do well academically was now implanted.

She gave me three gold stars for my report, the highest mark! I could see some of my classmates looking on enviously. I proudly shared my tale with my father when he returned from work. He beamed with pride; we both emerged victorious from our battle of wills the night before.

I was elated one day when my father was able to take time off work at Smith Industries to drive some of the team in his now up-graded Rover Coupé to the Barnet Borough six-a-side football tournament, which we won. This was the only time I recall my father ever attending a sporting or other event in which I was participating; other than my college graduation. He was a keen football fan and we suspect went surreptitiously to the odd league game; he was a closet supporter of The Gunners, Arsenal.

We watched the 1970 Mexico World Cup in our dining room crowded excitedly around our oversized dining table (which doubled as a Ping-Pong table when our parents were out). The tiny screen of our aging black and white television flickered on-and-off as we marveled at the dazzling skills displayed by the fabulous winning Brazilian squad led by Pele, Carlos Alberto, Jairzinho, Tostao, the left footed wonder Rivelino, Roberto and the comical goalkeeping antics of Felix. We took turns holding and adjusting the antenna to better capture the picture signal to bring the grainy Apollo-like images back on the screen.

Other happy moments included playing draughts, Ludo (Parcheesi), or Monopoly with my father and siblings with our own unique family rules designed to liven these otherwise boring board games. My mother did not participate, she was usually too exhausted from work and tending us and glad for some respite.

A tormented, disheveled, snot nosed boy at Dollis took it upon himself to liberate my Smith Industries watch bought with father's hard earned money while we were in the frigid pool for our twenty-five yard swimming test. A test I had dreaded for months. When I came home and told my father, he was less than amused and insisted on coming to school the next morning to meet with Mr. Clayton, the headmaster. Mr. Clayton's lame efforts to brush us off were not well received by my father:

"This man does not know who he is dealing with, he thinks we are fools."

"We will teach them a lesson."

The headmaster in effect implied that a white peer would not steal the watch of a black pupil. Some days later I saw the boy wearing the watch in the playground and approached him to return the watch. He refused and denied having purloined my watch, he had not been smart enough however to remove the distinctive green strap that I had put on the watch. I informed my father who said:

"In di ala, fa maro onye um bu (mad people, they don't know my mettle (who I am))."

"Anyi ga agba fa ose (we will light a fire under their behinds)."

"Fa amaro afufu m'talu we gotalu yi elekele-aka (they don't know what I suffered to buy you a watch)."

We returned the next day with a policeman and the boy apologized and returned the watch. There was however no apology from Mr. Clayton or indeed anyone else from the school. I was sorry for the boy. He was a military brat, the son of a squaddy (member of the British armed forces) at Inglish Barracks near Mill Hill East tube station. Father and I visited the boy's home with the policeman and guessed he was probably punished for his misdeeds. The family I subsequently found out was soon posted to a new unknown destination in the far-flung corner of the British Commonwealth. A triumph for British justice and its fair minded Bobbies once again! My father, despite the inequities we experienced, very much believed in justice, especially when it came to the rights of his children. For instance, when we lived in Kano father famously thrashed a teacher who took it upon himself to inflict corporal punishment on his children without the consent of my parents. This spirit of justice, I leaned many years later, prompted him to assist fleeing Ibo families escape Nigeria during the Biafra conflict. Father helped arrange surreptitious flights through various corridors in Nigeria's porous borders.

8. John Holt

Now well into adolescence, I still struggled to find my own voice to express myself and who I was. I was among other things unsure how much I could talk about my home life and the fact that we ate pounded yam with bitter leaf stew, and not dull fish and chips or baked beans on toast for dinner. Spoons, knives and forks were used only for cornflakes and other exotic Western dishes, like toad-in-the-hole, otherwise at home we washed our hands in a communal bowl and ate with our fingers, dipping our pounded yam in delicious pungent smelling soup dishes, like pepper soup, we all shared together around the dining table. Chores for setting the table were divided among my five siblings, my brother Nonso brought the bowl of water to wash our hands, and another fetched the kitchen towel to wipe our wet hands, while place mats were entrusted to yet another. My job was to bring a (recycled) bottle filled with ice-cold water from the fridge and drinking glasses. My elder sister, Augusta, meanwhile, helped my mum prepare dinner while the younger six year-old Chinwe looked on and learned how each dish was made. After the meal, we each said the customary respectful: "Thank Sir", to my father, and "Thank Ma", to my mother. At home we spoke Onitsha-Ibo and called each other by our Ibo names. Our inside identities were secret from our friends outside. We were all very close, and home was our world far removed from English or British life.

It was against this backdrop some months into my secondary school that my father assembled us one Saturday afternoon in the living room. He announced smiling, "I've been appointed second-in-command to the British General Manager for the travel business of John Holt", a major British trading concern in Nigeria and West Africa. There had been an expectant air in the household all morning ahead of the official announcement. Relieved it was not the sort of bad news about a deceased relative back in Nigeria that would send haunting howls from my sorrowful mother. I was cheered by the unexpected good news and was very glad my father would be leaving his droll troglodyte anonymity at Smith Industries for a position that would restore his self-esteem. This was a position he could be proud and passionate about. A job that could heal the humiliation and pain that almost broke him after dismissal from the Airways, and the losses brought on by the Biafra war. At the same time, once the initial euphoria wore off, I was both relieved and sad, relieved because I would not be subjected to my father's strict, watchful, and often critical eye, and sad he would not be around particularly for my football games. Father had a rascal quality which when at his best was a joy to be around.

As was the Onitsha democratic practice in our household, an impromptu forum was convened to decide who would return and who would stay. The sun, unusually for the time of year, shone brightly into the living room where we were assembled. Father spoke first, "My preference is for all of us to return together", he then asked, "Who wants to stay behind?" We all looked down at our navels and said, "Mba" (No). It was a resounding affirmative vote to stay in London and our schools. The thought of another disruptive move was too much for me to even contemplate. Readjusting to life in Nigeria would not be easy, so it was that my mother remained with us in London. Father notionally would visit throughout the year during his long leaves. This having been said, I think he was crushed this time round about the prospect of separation from his family again, however compelling the reasons were for his move and us remaining in London. He sensed that his children were slipping away from him and our Onitsha cultural roots. Father tried as best he could to sell the merits of a return to Nigeria and the charms of St. Gregory's, a prestigious private school in Lagos. "Your friend Daniel from Wessex Gardens goes to Saint Greg's", but at this juncture I had been won over by the idiosyncratic charms of Britain and her shores. For my part, youthful as I was I reasoned that having raped and pillaged our country and those of the former empire with reckless abandon, the least Britain could do was to extend a welcome in return. This was going to be re-colonization, so to speak, by the Udos.

A survivor, father rose quickly from the ashes like the proverbial phoenix and flourished in his new role, although he chaffed under the direction of his less experienced British boss. A situation that would lead him to buy-out John Holt travel at the first opportunity he had once the group announced its retreat to focus on other core businesses in West Africa. He rechristened the agency Roxy Travels and expanded quickly to make the firm the largest travel agent in Nigeria. He was once again in the public eye, and the window to the world for the country's rich and famous. An avid globetrotter, he became famed for venturing to the Soviet Union to win the exclusive travel rights for Nigerians to the 1980 Moscow Olympics. Father was fond of gadgets and I now understood the reason for the furiously late night typing, in carbon triplicate, on his prized blue ribbon portable Olivetti typewriter, some weeks earlier. Back in London, I had much to be proud about again about my father, which made his absence in some ways even more difficult.

A couple of years after our family meeting, my elder sister Augusta moved back to Nigeria to join Sammy and Lauretta in my father's home, after prophetically completing a cutting-edge key cards computer course. (Comfort was back teaching and had her own home). Augusta's presence brought stability to a crowded household of cousins and passing "aunties". In rebellion, at being marginalized in his father's home, my younger half-brother absconded from boarding school and went on a walkabout in search of attention from a busy father and a mother (Comfort) struggling to find her feet back in Nigeria. Sammy wanted to join the army which was a popular route to wealth and power then among his peers, but was forbidden to do so by my father. Given the tragedy of the Biafra war, the military, the business of killing foes, was seen by my father as a less than respectable occupation. Lauretta, my outspoken, jovial and larger-than-life half-sister, was also attending boarding school. While she welcomed Augusta's return, she was resentful of losing the mantel of the elder daughter in the household. Something I was familiar with myself having had the same experience with the return of my elder brother and other siblings to London in December 1966. This tension was a recurrent theme with my half-siblings Lauretta and Sammy, who were younger and as such had to show cultural deference to their older brothers and sisters, like me, but rightly also saw themselves as the eldest daughter and son of father's second wife. This latter position was also political since it conferred certain rights and privileges under local custom and law especially regarding inheritance.

Augusta later joined Union Bank, formerly Barclays, in Nigeria and worked for many years as a manager in their computer department. She also served as a union representative, which saw her jailed for a brief stint for defending worker rights against the interests of management. She explained that having seen the importance of worker's rights in radical 1970s England, she could not sit idly and watch struggling hard working subordinates endure inhumane treatment and abuse at the hands of an indifferent management. The genteel Dominican nuns in Dublin, Ireland, where she attended boarding school, had taught her well; to respect the rights and dignity of all.

It was my father's ambitions to have at least one son assume the helm at Roxy Travel; something alas none of us showed even the faintest of inclination in doing. Like my siblings, I preferred instead to chart my own course in life, free from father's critical eye. I missed Augusta, my beautiful sweet sister who the nuns had given a classical and practical prim-and-proper lady's education. It was Augusta who looked after us while mother was at work or grocery shopping. When she herself started work, like my mother, she would bring us ife afia (special market treats, e.g., biscuits), on pay day. We were tearful at her departure like that of Theresa earlier but the circumstances of her own life made it important that she return to Nigeria of her own accord having reached marriageable age. She knew also that her own departure would keep us connected to Nigeria and my father.

Our mother henceforth would have to learn to make ends meet, muddling through without Augusta's support and getting-by sometimes stretching out her negligible wages to buy school uniforms. I remember on more than one occasion being anxious and worried as I took home the school note to my mother with a list of uniform requirements and supplies for the new school year. Nigeria's foreign exchange restrictions and endemic corruption delayed or at times made it impossible for our family allowance from my father to turn up when expected. Mother slowly learned to manage her own finances and to chart her destiny and that of her children and to navigate the whys-and-wherefores of the British way of life, attending parent teacher nights for her children, trusting her children to do right and welcoming our friends into our new home while at the same time watchful that she did not once again become the fall-guy for any shortcomings as occurred with our unfortunate cousin Theresa. Even with my father in Nigeria, clashes continued as to how to bring up the children. She faced an enormous responsibility and countless often-unwarranted criticism from my father and his side of the family back in Onitsha. My elder brother's choice to leave school early and to start work as a management trainee at the August haberdashery firm of John Lewis's, the quintessential British retailer, was one such point of contention. I've always marveled at the remarkable partnership that is John Lewis, where workers are owners along with management and share many materially enriching amenities and privileges beyond the shop floor. Regi, in my father's absence felt compelled to work, to my father's consternation. Both my father and mother wanted him to go to university (college). Nigeria's declining economic fortune ironically brought the financial uncertainty that my father had returned to Nigeria to erase. I felt that Mother's task, in many respects, was a thankless one, save for the love and respect of her children and her own keen sense of survival and intelligence. Her often precarious plight was further exacerbated by the fact that like many other newcomers to the United Kingdom entering the workforce, she was open to exploitation by unscrupulous employers who frequently found excuses to deny immigrants pay raises and promotions ahead of their white colleagues. My mother tempered these experiences by explaining to me on the occasions I came face-to-face with blatant discrimination that: "This was not our country". This argument rang hollow especially as we grew older, assimilated, and ourselves began to seek employment and the bountiful opportunities created through British imperial conquests. Mother too had mellowed, abandoning the disciplinarian authoritarian Thatcher-like parenting style that marked our days in Lagos, which made often open and frank conversation on many delicate matters, like dating, now possible.

I would knock on mother's bedroom door after dinner when she would be resting. "Come in" she would say in a gentle reflective voice. I explained how I was mysteriously excluded from this or that school activity although I clearly merited selection. She listened quietly and then would say, "e sobuna, orga di ma, oboda aburo biayi, orgadi ma", (don't worry, this is not our country, all will be well). That was all that was needed to reassure that not all the world was bad and unfair.

Mother's dream marriage had been shattered even before it had really begun. She had to navigate the perils of new wives, none of whom stayed the course in an oftentimes difficult and sometimes tempestuous polygamous relationship. She endured a husband who was mostly away due to postings abroad during fifty plus years of precarious marriage. Her personal hopes and aspirations vanished prematurely as she surrendered to the drama of her complicated marriage. She was saddled with the difficult task of raising her remaining children and various wards, nephews and nieces, from my father's family. A strict disciplinarian in those early years, circumstances were such that she had little time to dole out demonstrative love to her children, particularly those like me, born after my elder brother Regi. She had little opportunity to recover from the triple emotional trauma of separation from her son Osi, the loss of Obiageli and then my unborn twin. Her father was distant, and her mother difficult. Women of her era were expected to stoically soldier on with token support from equally emotional and physically distant spouses. Support came mainly in the form of female relatives, neighbors, and family friends. Any chance at lavishing love on her children evaporated with the unset of the turmoil that preceded civil war. She acted instinctively to save her children, only to end up at the home of wife number two in London, in a less than harmonious arrangement in an inhospitable land far from home. These difficulties were exacerbated by an unhappy disillusioned husband, whose dramatically changed fortunes saw him transformed from the smart, charming, and fun loving man she knew and loved to someone frustrated with the vicissitudes of life.

The trilogy of loss in quick succession would drain any mother of emotion. Mother also had the trauma of war and death, layered on for good measure, on top of the domestic tension of new wives. My mother was unrewarded and underappreciated until my college years, when I had perspective to appreciate what she had suffered and sacrificed to give her children the best opportunity she could. Particularly poignant for me were memories of my mother at the checkpoint and later jostling among frightened Ibos at the Lagos inoculation center to complete all formalities that would see us safely out of Nigeria. Like many women of her time, she possessed a courageous will which enabled her to prevail seemingly at times against insurmountable odds with little physical or moral support. Courage at times seems to be the exclusive preserve of women.

It was not surprising then that I was closest to my mother during these years in Mill Hill where I saw her emerge as the head of our household in London. For the first time she had room for and to be herself. She guided her children in very difficult circumstances through adolescence in a very complex and alien culture that was far removed from her own experiences. She sublimated her own personal aspirations and desire for happiness for the success of her children, receiving little thanks and encouragement from an absent husband engrossed with his own challenges and preoccupations.

9. Finchley

Any lingering thoughts I had about belonging and feeling at home in England's mono-cultural class-ridden-society of the 1970s, would soon be answered in my years at Finchley. I waited anxiously and with some trepidation for school to begin. On my first day, I was glad to see amid the forest of pasty bleached white faces, the vague contours of the giant mountain, Charlie Etame, a fellow West African-Anglophone from the Cameroons. At seven years-old, Charlie and I were on opposite sides of a furiously contested football match for our respective primary schools. The outcome of the game, despite the "giant's" presence, was neutral. It was a 1-1 draw, which gave the basis for me to approach Charlie without fear of offending or causing embarrassment because we had won or lost.

"Hello" I said extending my diminutive hand which vanished within Charlie's enormous grip.

"Aren't you from Clitterhouse School?" "We played against you when I was at Wessex Garden".

"Yes" said Charlie gruffly, as if I had interrupted some deep metaphysical thought. My presence on the field had clearly been unremarkable for him.

This brief playground exchange was to be the start of a friendship spanning more than forty years. Culture shock awaited us in the corridors of the school. We had much work ahead of us to debunk popular misconceptions about those of color that lingered among certain pupils and students alike not fortunate enough to have met Africans first-hand. Meeting such individuals, I felt like Doctor Livingstone must have felt when he first encountered natives on "The Dark Continent". Mercifully, Charlie's intimidating physical bulk did much to temper any hostilities. His mere presence was often more than enough to quell any errant cheeky or abusive thoughts that could lead to racial taunts or misdeeds among our rowdy, boisterous, energetic, and inventive fellow pupils. His prodigious size gave pause for reflection and encouraged tolerance, even among the most dense and unenlightened pupils, "Bovver [bother] boys" intent on a "bit of agro" -- aggravation or violence, trouble in North London parlance.

It was at Finchley that I would complete my obligatory newcomers' apprenticeship. I learned to navigate between two divergent cultures, at home and outside, and to gingerly traverse those bathed in ignorance about who I was; often intent on doing harm, and in the process undermining my intellect, and spirit.

By the time I was eleven and ready to move onto secondary school, my father decided that my academic skills had improved to the point where we could apply to a selective church school, Finchley Catholic Grammar. He arranged an interview. Feeling somewhat petrified at having to do the interview with my father in the room, I sat across the desk from the elderly headmaster, Father Groves. The headmaster was a large man, about six feet tall, dressed in the black cassock uniform of his clerical profession with a white starched priest's collar, kindly eyes, monk like tonsure, and a gravelly voice that made you want to sit bolt-upright in his presence.

Father Groves leaned in. "What do you get if you multiple five by thirteen?"

I spat-out as quickly as the cogs in my head could calculate, "Sixty-five!" My legs pressed hard against his desk and I hoped to God that my answer was correct.

He smiled.

Finchley

"Do you know your times-tables and how to do long division?"

"Yes"

"Do you attend church and confession regularly?"

"Yes", I answered, even though I knew my piety was in doubt. I frequently had to make up sins at confession, which must have been a sin in-of-itself, in order not to sit in silence in the confessional with the priest behind the screen pondering my irritated state and fidgeting anxiously with his rosary.

After a few more math questions and some bantering about sports accomplishments at Wessex Gardens, Father Groves leaned back in his chair. He took a deep puff from his cigarette, exhaled the smoke in a long, impressive plume, and then briefly examined his nicotine-stained fingers. Finally he met my gaze.

"Welcome to Finchley", he said with a wry smile and the unspoken knowledge of an old fox.

"I expect that you will make a good addition to this year's intake of boys".

My father was elated! We left the head's office with a warm glow and copies of the school magazines Harvest and Tolley (which sounded more like a glossy magazine read by dirty old men in trench coats than a school's magazine) in our mitts; we thanked the school's often heroic secretary. Father no doubt viewed my favorable admission as recompense for my botched television audition some years earlier.

We were part of the first secondary school intake under what was dubbed "The New System". Pupils were above average intelligence. Finchley, an all boys' school was modeled after public (private) schools and in certain respects would not have been out of place in Tom Brown's School Days a grim novel by Thomas Hughes published in 1857, set at Rugby School, a public school for boys, in the 1830s. It was set in future Prime Minister Margaret Thatcher's constituency on several generous acres of land with neat trimmed lawns, gardens, and orchard fields which housed cricket nets for practice at the crease. Sixth and Seventh formers played croquet on their allotted lawns facing the Chemistry laboratories watched jealously by juniors fiddling with Bunsen burners and longing for the bell to be rung for the end of the school day at four-o'clock. All this while the Chemistry teacher, aptly named "Stinks" in the tradition of English schools and in part because of his flatulence problem, rambled on through the elements that make up The Periodic Table and with equal rigor the different valances of chemical elements. The buildings consisted of several modern blocks, an old miniature castle appositely named the "White House" modeled after an Etruscan Temple and no doubt a harbinger of my years to come in America (Old boys' Albanian Association-History; courtesy Conn O'Halpin, edited by Chris Parker). Various red brick Victorian houses circled the perimeter of the property, these former residences for boarders now served as the music house, sixth and seventh form houses as well as the attractive caretakers' lodge. There was an elaborate House system which matched off with different colored ties. Your House was determined by where your surname fell in the alphabet. I, along with others grouped "P" through "Z" were in Thomas Moore House which meant black and purple polyester ties. Charlie Etame, who was to become my oldest friend, was in Bourne, blue and black ties and so on. The Houses were named after famous ecclesiastic figures like Thomas Moore and Fisher, who stood up for the Catholic faith and for humanity in general. The latter, the Bishop of Rochester in Henry VIII's reign was condemned to death for loyalty to Pope Paul III. He was made a

Cardinal before his death to which Henry retorted with his own brand of caustic humor, "Paul may send him the red [Cardinal] hat, but I will see that he has no head on which to wear it" (Old boys' Albanian Association-History; courtesy Conn O'Halpin, edited by Chris Parker). Sports activities were organized along House lines. Despite being a Catholic School, the only clerics to be seen were the Headmaster Father Groves who soon retired and was replaced by the young lay Ned Kelly who on occasion donned boots and played footy with the boys on the school playing fields, Father O'Halloran a genial math buff (aka Holy Harry) and the dry and often humorless Cannon Ward. Cannon Ward or Doc Ward as he was known then is legend at the school. He was asked while teaching a class in an air-raid shelter during the war years "was that a bomb" dropping in the next street he replied "Yes!", "get on with your work" (Old boys' Albanian Association-History courtesy; Conn O'Halpin, edited by Chris Parker). He typified the stoic ethos of the school. Friday afternoon Benediction for scholars had long been abandoned but Chapel was required once a week. Save for Chapel and Religious Education (RE) we were largely left to our own religious devices. We had Church of England, Jewish and Muslim students and faculty attracted by the school's open philosophy and unique tradition typified by benefactors like Spike Milligan of Goon fame whose son attended the school. The school was divided into a lower school, middle school and the sixth and seventh form houses. Each was run as a fiefdom by its respective head; the religiously zealous head of the lower school ran the school with an iron rod and was universally feared by the students. We dreaded hearing three words: "Come here boy!" from the bald stern-faced Irish android, dressed in somber undertaker black with a white shirt and black tie. He made Hitler seem tame. His fanatical zeal was countered by the demure and soft-spoken co-Head who, being a nutty scientist himself, had a little more tolerance for the inventive pranks of energetic eleven and twelve year-olds. These pranks included balancing buckets of water on the top corner of the classroom door so that they toppled over and drench the teacher once he or she opened the door. I sadly cannot remember who ran the middle school. The sixth and seventh form houses were presided over by Sammy Hewson. Mr. Hewson, an energetic and engaging man, ran the houses like a ship. He encouraged the debating society, in which I was once asked by a teacher with an acute sense of wicked sinister humor: "Udo why don't you defend the apartheid system in debate today". I disturbingly won the debate! Under Mr. Hewson's guidance a flourishing tuck shop took root in the sixth form common room where students smoked fags (usually Woodbine roll-up cigarettes), played darts, talked politics, the merits of toxophily, football, the relative virtues of David Bowie, Genesis, and Pink Floyd's latest vinyl LP albums, St. Michael's girls (since those, other than our mothers' and sisters, were the only we knew), fishing, equine racing-form, and bookies-odds that evening at the dogs in White City. Boys however were expected to always be "ship-shape and Bristol fashion". Having presumed him long deceased, I was pleasantly surprised to come across Sammy Hewson and his wife at the school's seventy-fifth anniversary celebration in 2006. My surprise was not well concealed. A robust Mr. Hewson, sensing this, broke the ice with the refrain: "yes it's me Udo; I am still alive and looking forward to the school's hundredth anniversary in 2026!" Judging from his lively form, I should not at all be surprised to see him there at the age of ninety-six or thereabouts. On hearing the news many years earlier of my admission to Harvard, he quizzed "what about Oxford and Cambridge my boy?" "Those are fine academic institutions", as if I had sold myself desperately short by electing to attend Harvard a third rate academic institutions in the former colonies.

Pupils wore school uniform with yellow and blue braided jackets (originally azure and gold back in the day), white or grey shirts, grey trousers, black or charcoal socks and peaked school caps, a source of taunting and ridicule from neighboring school boys. Ties had to be tightly knotted with top buttons securely fastened. Penalties for failing to observe these protocols ranged from boxed ears, a brusque stinging slap delivered with deadly force across the chops, detention, to lines and kneeling for countless hours in some far flung corner of the school. The school motto was emblazoned on our caps: "Dan obis recta sapere" or "Grant that we may be always truly wise". The meaning had clearly failed to register on some of our more feloniously inclined pupils. Some of whom in contrast to their other reprobate activities were ardent in their devotion to charity work for the underprivileged and old people's causes. In a strange way, I liked Finchley's strict rules which were far less draconian and confining than one would have imagined in an equivalent school in Nigeria. You knew where you stood, and it was your choice to test or stray beyond the limits with its grave consequences.

Down the road was St. Michaels, the all-girls Catholic School that produced many unions and offspring between the two schools. It was there that I met the lovely Marie, a tall red haired Irish beauty who was my first steady girlfriend. This innocent romance would end abruptly when I announced I had been admitted to Harvard and was soon to be bound for Cambridge, Massachusetts. Her mother was a former nun and her father seemed equally saintly. He discreetly turned a blind eye when he discovered us half-naked entangled in an amorous embrace one school afternoon on their living room floor. We were supposedly "revising" (studying) for our upcoming A 'level exams.

The boys at Finchley had many other qualities which more than made up for our academic deficiencies: our razor wit, superior knowledge of footballing greats, match scores including those of the Scottish, Welsh, Irish, Italian, and Polish leagues, and encyclopedic knowledge of local pubs and other establishments of ill repute. We were exceptional at marbles, penny-up-the-wall, British Bulldog, and could act every Monty Python skit from memory verbatim as if reciting Shakespeare's Macbeth on stage in Regent's Park. The school drew a variety of gifted and variously talented Caribbean, English, Greek, Irish, Italian, Lithuanian, Polish, Scottish, Welsh and African boys, from all social classes and all corners of London including the strong Irish neighborhood Kilburn. Some travelled tens of miles to attend each day, commuting several hours on numerous buses and tubes in pursuit of a Catholic schooling.

The faculty included the towering and brilliant English teacher Denny O'Shea, a strict disciplinarian, with zero tolerance for insolent boys of limited intellect and only a passing love for English literature. I recall Denny O'Shea and the rebellious Rasta, Sylvester, dueling energetically as to the etymology of the word "niggardly" and its appropriateness for use in the modern classroom. Sylvester impolitely gesticulating, lips pursed, letting out a derisive sucking hiss and rant in Jamaican patois: "Raasclat".

Finchley

Denny O'Shea, unfamiliar with the etymology of the Jamaican word "raasclat" looked up confused, but dogged as ever, dug deep in his reservoir of literary history. He made a futile last attempt at sanity.

"Sylvester"

"The word "niggardly" has Shakespearean origins and has noting to do with the word "Nigger"!

"Niggardly means miser or stingy, its origins are traced to the Wycliffe Bible of 1384 when the word was spelt "nygard" or "nigan", and later in the sixteenth century became "niggard"."

"Sylvester, laddy"

"The word nigger is the Latin word for black from which "Nigger" is derived."

Sylvester was not moved by Mr. O'Shea's arguments and sat vexed and sulking in the back of the class.

There were a handful of children of color at the school and Sylvester was never shy to point out any actual or perceived slight. Race in the 1970s was an extremely thorny issue that was not easily discussed among the English. For me, race for the most part was a non-issue at school, in fact my white classmates were generally quick to energetically defend and physically fight against any slights or bigotry directed at me. This same spirit was not something I have found in abundance in America, an individualistic society where you take care of your own affairs and problems.

Other notable faculty members included an explosive and not to be provoked bicycling geographer who claimed to have been shot by Al Capone while in a Speakeasy in darkest America, a historian and football junky who legend has it passed away from a heart attack while watching his beloved Arsenal team in the FA Cup final, the stunning arts mistress who allegedly was found on the art room floor entangled with a sixth former, our diminutive Physical Education (PE) teacher who introduced us to the thrill of basketball, as well as gritty northern English culture. There were many others, colorful teachers, who graced the smoke-filled Finchley staff room during my years at the school. I loved the school, the esprit de corps among the motley staff, the old boys association, its values, teachers and pupils.

In my last two years at Finchley I became close friends with a group of pranksters who raided Sammy Hewson's office to liberate copies of our university letters of reference, the most amusing of which described one of our gang as "dandy in act" much to his annoyance. The young man's sartorial elegance was legend at the school. The most brilliant of our clique, Tim, won a prestigious management trainee scholarship with Cadbury after which he worked in London's fast moving commercial property market. He seemed destined for great things having also gotten engaged to the very beautiful and charming Dutch tulip Emma. I received a call one day from one of our gang who asked me to call Tim, but not to say who I was. I followed his directions and was greeted by an ebullient Tim who I discovered tragically had dashed his brains out while on a boys-only ski trip to Italy. Tim lost all his memory beyond our last year at Finchley! He was locked in a time warp. His long-term memory of college and his professional career was erased as a result of the accident and his short-term memory became precisely that, very short. While in a long induced coma, his sister, a farmer's wife, was deeply shaken by the tragic accident. Grief ridden thinking Tim was lost forever, she took her own life before he regained consciousness. Tim unaware of the circumstances of his sister's death visited New York

Finchley

with his mother having won a Timeout Magazine competition. During his visit, I asked if he was sad that Emma, his fiancée, had left him after the accident. He smiled and said: "not at all, it was odd waking up each morning with a complete stranger in your bed."

I now began to fully understand the rich tapestry of life and how capricious and fleeting it could be.

10. Sports and Athletics

The annual Sports Day was a big event at Finchley. It offered an opportunity for students to win laurels outside the classroom and to attain much prized "School Colors (Letters)". Given my athletic successes outside of the school House System, it was not the high point for me as it was for some of my peers, like Mario Francescotti. Mario the former head of Morgan Stanley in Asia was a rival in O'level economics in which we both gained "As". We were his guests at the patrician Shek O Golf Club in Hong Kong. It was there that Mario revealed that I caused untold grief when I relegated him to second place in the House high jump competition. "You put paid yet again to my ambitions for gold", a prize that clearly meant more than I had appreciated at the time. There was a special butterfly filled excitement competing on the hallowed cinders of the local stadium with lanes marked in white with lime and pupils cheering merrily from the stands in the midst of English summer drizzle. Teachers dashed about frantically to ensure straying javelins or shot-putts did not impale students, and offered pithy instructions as to how to propel these deadly implements. Being a gifted athlete, sporting success came very easily to me. I was far from arrogant, but I am embarrassed to say I never gave a second thought back then to the struggles or ambitions of others who were less sportingly gifted and for whom winning meant so much more. Whether in class or on the sports field, success became something I took for granted which was a distant cry from my unsure early youth. Through sports, I found a vocabulary to express myself, and to draw attention and sensitivity to who I actually was.

Sports and Athletics

I played football (soccer) and basketball and captained both teams. Sports were my window to the world. Participation in athletic pursuits vanquished fear and balanced ambition and youth for me. Sports brought with it lasting friendships, travel, discipline, and resolve to accomplish defined goals. Lessons and observations learned while playing sports would serve me well later in life. There was much to learn, for example, in an opponent's eyes, like fear or its complete absence. The latter crazed competitors typically feared neither God nor the devil. Some competitors played their cards very close to the vest; revealing only scant tale-tale clues in their warm-up as to their physical and mental condition. In some their thrash talking swaggering bravado, like those of the Skin Heads in the Isle of Wight, concealed fear and the knowledge that defeat was only moments away. Others like me had steely mental toughness and physical endurance that belied a demure appearance. Such prodigious talent spoke legend when unleashed. I still vividly remember my disciplined pre-match routine; laying out old newspapers on Friday nights to clean caked-mud and mold from my football (soccer) boots in preparation for 9:00 AM Saturday morning kickoff. The team travelled to match venues by coach (bus), younger pupils at the front and older senior pupils in the back seats usually smoking in a curious pre-match ritual. As a youngster you had opportunity to rub shoulders with senior (older) boys, particularly those who would soon be leaving to face the world outside. You were able vicariously, for those like me who were curious, to glimpse at the life that lay ahead for you.

I loved, on autumn (fall) mornings, seeing the dew from the night before on the grass and the crunching noise the pitch made under my studs on brisk frosty mornings. Our team was particularly talented and was Middlesex champions for the under-sixteen age group. We reached the quarterfinals of the national age competition, (London is geographically divided into two counties: Middlesex and London). My close friend Charlie Etame, a Cameroonian by birth, was a lavishly gifted player; he anchored both our fortress like defense and our athletics relay team. Charlie's father was a diplomat and I identified with his family's expatriate status and their achievement driven West African roots. Our friendship helped reduce my initial isolation at school. It was nice to have someone else around, other than my brothers Regi and Martin, to help counter the occasional profound ignorance and lack of knowledge about our home cultures and values.

Charlie was the first among my friends to own a car, a Mini, which with his sizable frame he would pick-up and lift into the smallest of London parking spaces. The Mini served to ferry us to the occasional social outing where passengers were careful not to lean on the moss and fungus covered windows in deference to their fashionable garb. Some very talented team members joined the ranks of apprentice professionals in the vain dream of progressing from the discipline of cleaning the boots of first team stars. Few teams escaped a drubbing from our magical eleven and there were many hard fought rivalries with the neighboring Catholic St. James School and the equally impressive and disciplined Cardinal Vaughan squad. Victories were celebrated in the All-together, a giant Roman like bath which accommodated the entire team, mud, sweat, and all. Manliness and standards of health and hygiene were rather different then.

My real passion was track and field at which I excelled, holding national age group records in long jump for almost a decade. Unlike soccer and other team sports, I loved the Zen effort and precision of track. Every sinew in your body had to be finely tuned for optimal performance. Months of rigorous preparation, physical and mental, boiled down to a short dash and leap. Beyond peeling-off your tracksuit, you were focused on a single goal, the exhilarating pleasure of simply jumping further than any other competitor on the day or running faster to breast the tape at the finish line. No physical contact was required, just you and your competitors against the elements, gravity, and your physiological limitations. In amateur track your performance was unadulterated and immutable. The sport also had the added advantage of much larger and varied teams both in sex, age, and ability. As I progressed in the athletics rankings it also offered an opportunity to travel and to meet people from many places, not just in the U.K. but from around the world. This included unlikely locations like Malta in the Mediterranean. In short, it was a window to an extraordinary education I could not have gotten in the classroom alone. Sports were part of my cultural journey to discovering who I was. Sports opened a whole new world of diverse humanity through which I discovered I was not alone straddling cultures. In England, cultural differences and accents, like race in America, were always alive, straddling north-and-south, as well as across foreign frontiers. These differences were, however, less insidious and hateful.

    I had the honor of captaining the county's team at the English School's Championships held at Copthall Stadium in Hendon in 1977, where I met the future Prime Minister Margaret Thatcher, then Tory Member of Parliament (MP) for Finchley and Princess Margaret who was discernibly groggy from an all-night party with her boyfriend Roddy Llewellyn, if the morning's tabloids were to be believed. Mrs. Thatcher said the same thing to all the team captains including some of the women captains, "How are you little boy" accompanied by a vigorous bone rattling handshake. I was sufficiently talented to be asked to join renowned Olympic coach Malcolm Arnold's elite squad, but I did not want to live the monastic existence of a semi-professional athlete following a singular pursuit of Olympic gold at the expense of all else. Arnold knew those with what it takes, but from my vantage point, there were too many compromises required at my still tender age even with the fame and fortune that Olympic gold apparently promised. The limelight for me was not the reason I participated in athletics and sports.

I competed with the likes of Daley Thomson two time Olympic decathlon champion, and represented England at senior level and Great Britain (GB) at junior level in West Germany against West Germany and the U.S.A. in 1978. On which occasion having boarded the ferry to Bremerhaven en route to compete in Lubeck, the venue for our meet, I produced my green Nigerian passport for onboard inspection by the captain. The GB team manager was mortified to see I did not yet possess a British passport. "Udo where is your British Passport?" This was a gross inexcusable oversight on my part typical for a preoccupied teenager. With classic English aplomb and diplomacy the team manager persuaded the ship's captain nevertheless to permit my clandestine entry into West Germany without a visa, admittedly under the protection of the British realm and a promise to present me to the same ship's captain on the return journey home. Mission accomplished, I then proceeded to sprain my ankle in a pothole in the warm-up area before the actual competition and was only able to manage a couple of

Sports and Athletics

painful under par jumps well short of my 7.59w meter English School record set some weeks earlier. That jump had left me two inches short of the Olympic qualifying standard for the Moscow Olympics. I watched the rest of the meet from the sidelines in awe. I witnessed the full might of the American athletics juggernaut demolishing our team. They produced some breathtaking sprinting and jumping performances hitherto unseen by European teens or indeed adults judging from the incredulous expression on the GB team manger's face.

I never got around to taking up the British Athletics Association's kind offer to expedite my British passport which I regretted years later when I returned from college in America to discover that Margaret Thatcher's government had rewritten the rules for nationality. The new rules effectively precluding those like me, who although long-time residents were pursing studies abroad and could no longer satisfy the test for actual minimum 270 consecutive days resident in the U.K. required for naturalization.

Through the club's auspices, the generous support of the local council, and the sponsorship of various local businesses, I secured a summer position working as a grounds man, mixing concrete like an alchemist in precise formulaic proportions of water, aggregate, sand, and cement. We picked pebbles from the numerous cricket fields and installed tarmac and concrete paths throughout the facility grounds. I also managed to demolish the brick supports for the gates to our work facilities while trying to maneuver a JCB tractor machine and trailer through the gates on a bet with my fellow laborers. Our motley donkey jacket clad crew included the stoic hard saving Indian John and Paddy John, the diminutive and extremely entertaining Irishman. The latter led my friend Charlie and me to believe he was our foreman. This was before we discovered he was supposed to be digging ditches along with us not gazing at the skies enjoying a cigarette while balanced on his idle spade barking instructions at us. The ever inquisitive Paddy John asked Charlie in his distinctive vernacular Limerick brogue: "will ya explain to me in a nutshell how the fecking radio and television work". This to reassure himself that the owners of the voices he heard and faces he saw were not actually locked in the devices. Charlie, unwearied and generous of heart as always, obliged with a précis on Marconi's invention since he was studying computer science at London University. Paddy John we were told one morning had stumbled down the stairs at home and was found dead by his wife.

I progressed the next summer to become the coach for the Borough's athletics program for young school children aged seven to eighteen at Copthall Stadium across the road from our home. I enjoyed this immensely and I found the program very rewarding for pupils and teacher alike. I learned patience from the latter job and an appreciation for the virtues of manual labor and those engaged in its pursuit from the former. Both jobs offered other more earthly rewards in the form of a small pay packet at the end of each month.

My athletics exploits brought with them a very small following of female groupies, in fact two to be precise. They were an unlikely pair, one petite, energetic, dark haired, and somewhat squat, and the other a tall skinny vapid blond who was soon married at seventeen. Both were from the neighboring and less than cerebral county school. They were a true study in contrast. My groupies were to be found smiling and cheering at most of my school competitions, flirting

Sports and Athletics

and eager to rub shoulders with a hometown hero who was regularly featured in the local district rag (newspaper paper). They had adolescent crushes that were normally reserved for pop idols like the Babe City Rollers. There ended the similarities, because my regimented athletic life left no time for dalliance with groupies, not even vapid ones. While at the English Schools Championships in Shrewsbury I drew the attention of an older pretty, bright, and athletic 100-meter hurdler whose charms were frustratingly lost on me. By the time it registered that this intelligent good looking young lady was keen to be in my company, it was time to return by coach (bus) down the M40 motorway to disperse to our abodes scattered throughout London. This left the longing hope of a chance meeting at an athletics (track) competition later in the summer when the passion of the moment may well have cooled or more likely the case the boyfriend would be back on the scene.

It was through athletics that my academic and travel interest grew. I was a member of Shaftesbury Harriers a local track club that featured Harvard, University of London, Oxbridge and other university graduates. On our numerous coach (bus) trips across the British Isles to Brighton, Cardiff, Cosford, Edinburgh, Kirby and France, to various club competitions, we talked about many subjects. These topics ranged from politics, science and economics to wine, reggae music, women, film, football, and rugby. In France I had a near death experience, almost drowning at a municipal swimming pool. I was about fourteen years old and the trip organizers somehow had forgotten to arrange for accommodation for us with the French families we were, like wartime soldiers, supposed to be billeted with. Weary from our long ferry and bus ride we were offered accommodation at the stadium where we were due to compete a day-or-two hence and access to the shower facilities in the indoor swimming pool. This meant as a practical matter sleeping outside on the foam high jump and pool vault mats.

Youthful as we were, none of our party requested rooms at the Hôtel de Crillon or Hôtel Le Bristol in protest; I for one was excited at the prospect of sleeping for the first time under the stars. We slept outside with the constellations above and resourcefully pretended to be workers at a local Renault car factory to gain access to their subsidized canteen. We bought baguettes and a couple of packets of butter to share among us like Brazilian Street urchins for breakfast, followed by delicious cups of French coffee from the local café. We took in the Louvre Museum and other places of interest and culture riding the metro and the city's now long gone single-deck buses where the back was open to the elements for smokers to take a puff and admire the beauty and magnificence of the City of Light.

One afternoon we were fooling around by the pool when I announced, "I can barely swim but a few yards", in disbelief and youthful antics my teammates pushed me into the deep-end of the pool. I can confirm that a drowning man does see the best moments of his or her life flash rapidly past in the flash seconds as they contemplate the lights permanently going-out. Looking up I could see my teammates laughing through the ripples in the water clearly believing I was pretending to be drowning. Finally after what seemed like an eternity, one of them, I cannot remember who, by merest luck sprung to life and plunged into the pool to rescue me from probable death by misadventure. After this experience I saw the world very differently and resolved to enjoy each day of

Sports and Athletics

life as much as possible and at some point to resume swimming lessons long abandoned after my frigid exploits at Wessex Gardens.

This was the beginning of my love affair with France. The magic and torrid excitement of this first exhilarating visit to Paris was only rivaled years later when I was introduced to France Télécom's fabulous and very civilized Minitel, a precursor to today's internet. Minitel's avant-garde service was contained in a sleek black box, which proclaimed France's modernity and sexy inventiveness to the world. Its miniature keyboard was the gateway to the phone directory, restaurants, train reservations on the Train à Grande Vitesse (TGV), and even online shopping. Like Paris, it was dark chocolate in an elegant gift-wrapped box, waiting for the world to discover and to catch-up.

Edinburgh was my favorite destination; we lodged at the local and very bohemian YMCA near the main Waverley train station. It had carpets caked with years of dust and other decaying matter which we gingerly navigated around. These minor inconveniences were more than made up for by the unbeatable price of several quid (British pounds) a night including breakfast of tea and buttered toast, no haggis alas. We woke early to walk through the beautiful morning mist literally miles across the hills and dales to Meadowbank to compete. Happy memories, these were true halcyon days of innocent youth.

11. Lagos

I found my mother one day in her bedroom busily sorting and organizing clippings from the sports section of the newspapers about me. I am not sure why, but in a fit of teenage hubris, I admonished her for what I must have thought was idolatry worship for collecting the clippings from the local and national papers. I had not realized she had been doing so over these many years. I had not appreciated just how proud she was of her son. She was clearly very upset, particularly since I asked her to throw the clippings away. Wounded she did. This was the end of her scrapbook, which of course I regret today. My behavior unfortunately was typical of the sultry, uncommunicative, insensitive behavior and the raw deal mothers often receive from teenage children. Testosterone charged I was perhaps too eager to cut mother-son intimacy for the world beyond.

Independent, headstrong and fiercely proud, mother has been far more successful than my father at un-tethering herself from the yolk of Onitsha; moving on, and assimilating in English society, to a degree I would not have imagined and certainly strangely beyond my own assimilation. Initially in the shadows, mother was motivated by love and was left to hold the family together.

I visited my father in Nigeria most summers, with some or all of my siblings and my mother, from the age of about fifteen to my early twenties, and had to deal with the culture shock of re-familiarizing myself with the local landscape, customs, and the expectation that I would one day return. The gang that I grew up with was now long gone or had lives far removed from mine. I was once again in the developing world, and the creature comforts of light and clean running water that I took for granted in England were luxuries that few had in Nigeria. By equal token I was in a place where my belonging was not questioned. A vast network of relatives was ready to embrace and welcome me with unquestioned love and understanding.

The country had changed considerably from the sixties; the imposing Murtala Muhammed Airport, named after a slain head of state, had replaced sleepy Ikeja airport. On arrival you were met by overpowering humidity and heat since despite the newness of the ultra-modern airport, the air-conditioning system did not actually work. Passengers milled around chaotically with numerous dubious looking touts sporting a variety of official and unofficial identification badges purporting to provide one service or another. All without exception were seeking to take charge of your documents for a "fee" to facilitate processing through the complex formalities of immigration and customs. The airport resembled Dante's inferno, airport officials were often in cahoots with the touts and passengers jostled to keep control of their documents and luggage which if they were lucky would arrive intact unmolested after an hour or more of waiting in the over-powering heat. For some their luggage did not arrive at all having been plundered and discarded by the luggage personnel who had reasoned that they had better use for the contents than the owner. Those fortunate enough to be "Big Men" or Ogas were met by a host of helpers who whisked them and their bags through customs and immigrations without the necessity for any official formalities. The immigration officers would greet passengers with the feared question "Oga what do you have for me?" before proceeding to strip those passengers unwilling to pass over "dash" (a gift, tip, or bribe), of anything of value, watches, cameras, jewelry, and foreign currency. Passengers emerged from arrivals relieved to have survived the buffeting only to realize they now had to play Russian roulette in selecting a safe taxi that would not leave them naked, bereft of remaining luggage and valuables at the side of the pothole filled expressway. Those less fortunate to run into desperate ruthless bandits on occasion paid with their lives or perished in the numerous car crashes that were the bane of travelers throughout metropolitan Nigeria. Arriving in Nigeria required great patience and an immeasurable sense of humor if you were to survive this gauntlet of hapless avaricious humanity. Luckily for us, we were usually met by personnel from Roxy Travel who escorted us through the formality of immigrations and customs to our waiting car with driver ready to race us home without stopping at check-points or red lights for fear of police, soldiers or bandits. Once we were home in our flat in Mainland Lagos, the house boy would prepare a meal of plantains, yam and stew followed by tea from my father's secret stash in his bedroom. Then, it was on to debriefing with resident or visiting cousins eager to bring us up to-date on the comings and goings-on in Mr. Udo's household. We would receive an update on whether business was flourishing or waning, which mistress was now in favor and broader family disputes raging back in Onitsha. Sometimes the conversation would touch on some of the up-to-the-minute political intrigues and exploits of the legendary prolific musician Fela Anikulapo Ransome-Kuti an adversary and firm critic of the military government and his self-declared Kalakuta republic, a commune in the heart of Mainland Lagos where all-night performances would take place at his Shrine nightclub. It was at the Shrine that clashes took place with the aptly called "Kill-and-Go" soldiers and military-police that raped guests and tossed his mother out of a top floor window in hopes of silencing Fela's vocal musical protests.

Our cousins made playful fun of our Oyibo accents and peculiar Western habits. "Ah, why are you drinking tea like Englishmen in a tropical Lagos". Depending on the time of year, the temperature often reached beyond a 100 degrees Fahrenheit! The sights and sounds of early morning Lagos would wake me up the next day, cockerels screeching, car horns blearing, Hausa maigadi watchmen squatting in the shade to defecate in open gutters, Yoruba music beating, and the pulsating sound of human chatter, Ẹ kú àáro ("good morning" in Yoruba) being repeated amid a sea of vibrant colors and laughter. I am not sure if it is my imagination but people in Nigeria laugh much more than almost anywhere else I know, certainly more than in England and America. Despite the stresses and tensions of material deprivation and crowded congested urban living, there is always a vibrant current of playfulness and laughter almost everywhere you go including the most unlikely hovels. Such laughter and accompanying smiling faces helped eclipse the poignant stench of open sewers.

Even with its sometimes-material inconveniences, visiting Nigeria was an exotic adventure. There seemed to be no bounds to opportunity in every form possible whether culturally or economically. The country was in the midst of a massive upward trajectory, in an oil boom-and-bust cycle in which billions of dollars would eventually evaporate in wasteful government spending and Swiss bank accounts. Such was the rapid pace of booming construction that hundreds of ships were anchored off Nigeria's congested Apapa Wharf port in Lagos unable to unload the quantum of cement, consumables, and other conspicuous luxuries being imported. Many foreign and local multi-millionaires were created overnight by the demurrage charges accumulated by ship-owners by merely waiting for months to berth and unload their vessels. A network of impressive elevated highways, some leading nowhere emerged in Lagos besides white elephants like a state-of-the-art incineration plant with no power supply to drive its turbines. It would be eventually dismantled for scrap. The imposing National Arts Theater shaped like a military cap stood at the center like a gem amidst the cauldron of rapid teaming and largely unplanned and uncoordinated urban chaos. Petrodollars flowed freely and there was an air of Shangri-La that bathed Nigerians at home and abroad with Herculean confidence. Strivers abounded in Lagos and those who stood still were likely to quench with hunger and thirst.

Meanwhile father's business prospered and annual turnover quickly eclipsed several million pounds sterling. This attracted the attention of a host of family and other hangers-on, as well as aspirant would-be wives. But oil prices declined rapidly and the economy came to an abrupt halt, which sent Roxy Travel and many other businesses dependent on discretionary spending spinning out of control. Some of these businesses including father's crashed, hemorrhaging uncontrollably. New exchange controls rendered travel increasingly difficult for Nigerians. The wanderlust of the country's elite and emerging middle-class accustomed to frequent foreign travel and holidays abroad evaporated almost overnight.

Father diversified his portfolio into local real estate in Enugu and assembled a fleet of Mercedes cars and other vehicles as a hedge against devaluation while some of his compatriots with less of a blind devotion to Nigeria moved their money abroad, buying property in London and elsewhere. Father, soon followed suit, he made funds available for a deposit to buy our house in Mill Hill, which was being privatized under the U.K.'s Thatcher economic reforms. This was his only concession to the massive economic changes that were to come in Nigeria. Roxy Travel steadily declined and folded by the end of the early nineties; pillaged of ticket stock by dishonest employees and their accomplices, which led to the loss of its International Air Transport Association (IATA) license. Father pursued some consulting work on various new airline ventures including exploring opportunities with Sir Freddie Laker of Skytrain fame, a UK charter entrepreneur who blazed the path for Sir Richard Branson's Virgin Airways and discount carriers like Ryan Air. Exhausted and exasperated with the county's ever changing currency controls, father retired to our house in Onitsha to breed dogs and raise chickens and turkeys and to live off the rent from his properties in the village and the boys' quarters in our main compound. He later took the prized Ozo title and became known by the honorific name Nnabuenyi (father is greatness) that marked his full transition back into the local culture and the Onitsha community he so loved and hankered for. Ozo titles are elaborate affairs where recipients disgorge accumulated personal wealth to the community for the privilege of communal recognition; a spiritual cleansing of sorts. In contrast to the world of Oyibos, communal not individual wealth is deemed the pinnacle of social status. He was wounded that his children and first wife did not attend the Iti Obi Ceremony (traditional embrace that is part of the Ozo ceremony, which can be by-passed if the title taker pays a fine. The fine goes to the communal purse of the Ozo titled men) and wondered if we were lost forever. The significance of the ceremony was lost on Nnabuenyi's now Westernized children; we did not understand its importance for my father and its significance for the birth and renewal of the Udo family.

Lagos, a city of several hundred thousand in the fifties was now a mega polis with a population exceeding 10 million people, congested and chocked with traffic so much so that the military government had to introduce an odd and even license plate regime for cars on the roads on alternate days. Wealthy Lagosians, true to form, flaunted this rule by simply buying two or more cars for the different days of the week making congestion and pollution even worse. Those caught violating the rules were unceremoniously whipped in full public gaze by the military, a sad sight as one watched respectable grown men in suits and flowing agbadas made to weep in the noon day sun.

To break the tedium of staying in my father's flat, listless on his plastic covered sofas that clung to you with the oppressive humidity, we would sometimes be driven by one of our drivers to his office, on Broad Street in the commercial district of town. There we shopped or went sight-seeing. A favorite destination was the National Museum where I searched empty display cabinets for long plundered antiquities. These tourist excursions annoyed father's drivers and meant as a practical matter interrupted opportunities to go AWOL (military term for someone absent without leave), usually to make illicit passenger pick-ups to supplement their meager salaries; or simply to visit with girlfriends dotted around town.

Father's office was a typical Lagosian affair, with rows of desks and busily typing secretaries on one side and sleeping clerks on the other. Files were piled about the office. Arabic gum was to be found on every desk along with BIC pens, discolored flight agendas, holiday brochures for various airlines and destinations. Ticket stocks were kept in father's office safe (an oxymoron as with many things in Lagos). Customers sat patiently crowded into every nook and cranny in the tight office space as florescent lights flickered on-and-off and ceiling fans whirled. If we made the mistake of leaving too early or too late, we would be stuck in the hell that was Lagos's "go-slow" traffic jams. Young and old hawkers of every shape and size descended on the highway to sell wears of all manners. The din of racing overheating car engines and chocking exhaust fumes was punctuated by a cacophony of unrelenting car horns. This was accompanied by cascading cries, some beyond human ingenuity and imagination: "battery!", "carburetor!", "fan belt!", "groundnuts!", "newspaper!", "Pepsi!", "sunglasses!", "water!", "watch!", "waterproof!", "petrol!", in short, all essential conveniences necessary for daily existence in a teaming bustling Lagos. Hawkers chased drivers to collect payments and passengers screamed for "change!" as traffic lurched violently forward before coming to a sudden halt. Hawkers were sent scurrying like rats as the sound of military police sirens filled the air announcing the approach of the soldierly head-of-state's cavalcade. Soldiers with guns and whips sliced a path through busy traffic like a hot knife through butter. Those who resisted or inadvertently blocked the president's path were severely and brutally dealt with by heavily armed soldiers hanging menacingly from the speeding convoy of vehicles banging on bonnets (hoods) warning drivers to clear a path. Those brave and or foolhardy enough to dive into the path created by the motorcade kept a respectful distance from the military vehicles to protect their lives and those of their passengers. They had to be equally careful not to run over scrambling hawkers or stray off the highway onto a section with a dead-end and an unannounced precipitous plunge into the shacks below.

From the looping and twisting 12 kilometer long Third Mainland Bridge you could see the residents of Makoko, a vast slum built on stilts down below in the lagoon, going about their business fishing with nets or moving timber in their canoes from nearby sawmills spewing wood-smoke, untreated chemicals and other pollutants into the lagoon and the surrounding air. Pedestrians darted furtively across the highway with complete and utter disregard for their own lives. Slaughter of the most truculent character was a daily occurrence as evidenced by the occasional mangled corpse on the roadside. Some pedestrians, unfortunate victims of molues (rusty decrepit Lorries (trucks) lumbering along on wobbly threadbare tires like old rouge elephants) suffered a slow painful death as a result of contracting tetanus from their injuries. On occasion frustrated rebellious drivers caused chaos by driving headlong against traffic turning the rules of the road upside-down and endangering the lives of drivers and pedestrians alike. At points en route home, the molding buildings of the once impressive campus of Lagos University Teaching Hospital (LUTH) where my playboy cousin Tony had studied and qualified as a doctor were also visible.

Despite the decadence and decay, there was an excitement and vibrancy about Lagos that resembled New York in its heyday. Money flowed and change disguised as progress was in abundance everywhere. Even Onitsha was alive with petrodollars. I witnessed this as another younger lawyer cousin named Tony drove me around in my wealthy uncle's dilapidated Volkswagen (VW) Beetle. We stopped at a booker (shack) restaurant on the banks of The River Niger.

There we ate delicious pepper soup with chunky zesty pieces of azu ndu (fish of life), washed down with several large bottles of ice-cold Star beer. Later in the evening we enjoyed peanuts in cones made out of old torn newspapers as we mingled with native sons and daughters returning from across the globe during Christmas to see their families, party, and to meet their future husbands and wives. They were home on holiday from pursuing various studies and respectable occupations abroad, as a prelude to returning in the hope of securing a senior official government post. Such post, of course, preferably in the oil ministry or as special assistant to the oil minister. I enjoyed my holiday trips to Nigeria but they left me pondering where home was for me, whether England or Nigeria? Nigeria was warmer and more exciting but also very chaotic, unpredictable, and tinged with complex extended family demands and loyalties that I was now becoming unaccustomed to.

On the way to Onitsha, father having left ahead of us, our driver Austin, a worthy NASCAR challenger or Formula One driver, raced at well over 200 kilometers per hour (124 miles an hour), along the long stretches of newly paved tarmac highways built through the lush rainforest. He was blissfully unaware of his precious cargo of my siblings and me. Austin decelerated to traverse thick muscular basking snakes leisurely slithering across the road while at the same time dodging immense potholes caused by flash floods and overloaded trucks. These rickety trucks were usually painted with bright religious motifs that extolled life while their somnolent drivers reckoned with headlong traffic slouched perilously over giant black shining steering wheels with emasculated sounding horns. Tattered police officers with aged rusty rifles at state border check-points with hungry toothy smiles were greeted with the local playful refrain in Pidgin: "Oga", "How di-go-di-go?" as palms were pressed in laughter Naira notes slipping from-one-palm-to-the-other, greased to ensure unmolested passage. The Hausa phrase: "Akawo Ba Wuli se Dogo Wombo" (He has nothing but his long dress [shirt or gown]) best describes the plight of most Nigerian policemen and women. We stopped at vast roadside markets where yams, plantains, and other freshly harvested food supplies could be bought. The rich and fertile red soil stained my sweat-soaked clothing and clung to my slippers. Vendors rushed to offer bush meat, razor-cutters (giant rodent like creatures), considered a delicacy on huge banana leaves as well as an assortment of other similar unidentifiable offerings. I loved these stops in the tropical savanna where the air was filled by Nigeria's many local languages and dialects. The earth's natural beauty, trees, vines, tropical birds, and other creatures human and otherwise at once surrounded you. Intermittent island settlements dotted the lush forest landscape where mankind co-existed with nature; birds chattered up above in the rainforest canopy and below women pounded cassava and yam rhythmically in pestles with infants on their backs safely held by their wrappers.

Once in Onitsha we visited various aunts, uncles, and cousins. If I was successful in persuading my father, we would visit my grandmother with whom he had a difficult relationship which I suspected had something to do with his earlier decision to take a second wife. Visiting my grandmother was always special, she lived in a house built by her father in the heart of our village with a courtyard, open veranda and roof decked with corrugated metal or bam-bam as it is known locally. In the rainy season the heavy rains played melodies on the bam-bam, which soothed the tedium of being inside. The house had no electricity or running water and showers were taken in the back from zinc pales some distance from the outhouse. You entered the house by ascending several stairs before descending into her parlor or living room where I sat the last time I saw her. The silver painted mud seats that circled the room were covered with batik and cushions. She greeted me with a joyous surprised cry, Kedu ("Hello"). Followed by a warm embrace and shouts of Chukwu Dalu! (Thank God!), as her eyes searched the heavens. This brought neighbors running in. Granny, as we affectionately called her, offered us soft drinks and called one of the many children running snot-nosed and half-naked in the compound to go and buy drinks from a nearby street stand. She spoke very little English and we talked in Ibo. "Granny why do you not have a television"? Her face beamed with joy as she proudly pointed to the pictures of her many grandchildren hanging on the walls of her living room and said in Ibo, "This is my television." I admired and respected her desire to keep life uncomplicated and uncluttered, preferring instead to enjoy what little remnants there were of the village life she knew as a child. This was a lively communal life with frequent neighborly visits with no thoughts of convenience or inconvenience. There was a healthy respectful bias toward the aged, what mattered most was togetherness and family, taking care of your own frivolous needs was an oxymoron. I visited again at my father's burial ceremonies to pay my respects to her spirit. The house was occupied by northern Hausa tenants and there were even more children in the compound. She was buried at her father's house in Ogbeabu village in Onitsha, the same village that Nigeria's first president Zik was from. I have always been curious about the childhood lives of my parents and various close relatives since I grew up in a world very different from their own. I did not experience the colonial vestiges that shaped their lives and their encounters with Europeans in Nigeria. For them it was the Europeans who often struggled to become accustomed to the rhythm of local life, where for me it was the opposite living abroad.

By necessity of circumstance, I became adroit at managing the tensions between my Nigerian and English backgrounds. I was at once functional in Onitsha-Ibo, Pidgin, cockney rhyming slang, and BBC English. I was sufficiently inculcated in Onitsha-Ibo customs, and Lagos slang to be recognized as Nigerian, but yet familiar with arcane English cultural traits and turns-of-phrase which were undeniably germane to a native Englander bred in North London. I developed identities, which fitted comfortably in both cultures and moved easily between the two. To my Onitsha relatives, I am and remain Azubike or Ike, and to my English friends, I was Gus. In some instances those I encountered in England knew little of my two selves, facsimiles of the same person, opposite sides of the same coin. This duality would assume new levels of complexity with my choice to settle in New York and to become an American.

PART III: New Pastures: 1979-Present

12. Harvard

My time at Harvard felt like Huckleberry Finn's journey down the river. I had many exciting and new encounters and gained a welcomed insight and cursive understanding for America. This was my introductory level course; a 101 elective on America and its peculiar and extraordinarily enthusiastic citizens "across the [Atlantic] pond". Harvard was a place where I had freedom to unify my two conflicted identities through the medium of a third, America. Campus life for the most part was cocooned from the world outside and I found O_2 (Oxygen) in abundance to contemplate the juxtaposition of my Nigerian-British heritage. It was a perfect setting for growth, learning, and civilized social discourse. I felt as if the world had been placed at my feet. I had been given the opportunity I had long craved to explore and test the limits of my boundaries. Unlike England, Americans were very keen, perhaps overly so, to enquire about differences. My English accent prompted daily repeated questions of:

"Where are you from?" "You have a quaint accent." All said with the appropriate American inflection or twang.

"Kansas"
"Vermont"
"Australia?"
"South Africa?"
"Canada?"

They were curious, and for the most part, uniformly unable to decipher the conundrum of where I actually was from.

My Harvard career began with two entry interviews, one with Dudley Fishburn, Editor of The Economist magazine and the other with Seamus Malin, the Dean for Foreign Admissions. Urbane and erudite,

Harvard

Dudley appeared supportive and encouraging of my application to Harvard. The interview with Seamus Malin, if I recall correctly was conducted in the lounge of the Russell Hotel in London where Seamus invited me to watch a European Cup football match. In this crowded but disarming and relaxed venue, Seamus, a seasoned veteran of the admissions office preceded to fire testing questions between goals and the half-time break, probing as to the seriousness of my intent and ability to a) survive and b) excel under Harvard's rigorous curriculum and its disciplined and talented community. I responded to Seamus that I was confident, which I was, that I would do well at Harvard. I was a born leader and had proven after some sub-par grades in my O'level year, at the age of sixteen, when my sporting activities were at their peak that given the opportunity I could excel. Finchley rightly or wrongly had pushed me hard to compete in football (soccer), basketball, athletics (track & field) and academics which left little balance in my life but did much to sharpen my poise, intellect, and leadership qualities.

Seamus, I later discovered had a second job; he was also a soccer commentator for one of the major networks which explained his choice of setting for the interview. I did not realize this that Harvard was seeking smart confident leaders which Seamus saw in me. These I am sure were leaders with a Capital (Uppercase) "L" that were more-or-less genetically pre-coded, engineered for success under Harvard's coveted formula. Before the interview I had flung myself without any preparation to speak of into the alien and perplexing world of SATs with mixed results, being unaccustomed to the rigors of multiple choice testing in a cold dank school hall at the American School in Hampstead, London. The day soon came when the nervously awaited admissions envelope arrived in the post with a heavy thud on the carpet below. I raced downstairs from the bedroom I shared with my brother Martin. Heart pounding I opened the envelope and found a letter and Certificate of Admission. I was at once elated and relived. Against the wise counsel from Dudley Fisburn, in typical reckless teenage fashion, I had narrowed my Ivy League college application choices to Harvard alone. Being oblivious of the competitiveness of the Ivy League application process and the dire odds I had placed against myself by applying solely to Harvard. Congratulatory calls followed from the track assistant coach Edgar B. Stowell who seemed even happier than I was on hearing the news. Harvard admission for me was less a case of the Holy Grail than an opportunity to leave England's confined shores. I wanted to be in a place less stodgy that recognized and rewarded talent without account for class, ethnicity or nationality. Nigeria's unpredictable economic and political fortunes made it a non-starter. I hankered after an environment free from cultural straightjackets, away from Britain's dreary, threadbare, 1970s subfusct. This was the extent of my American dream. How America actually measured up in reality would prove somewhat different.

Reflecting back to those breezy innocent days, ensconced in Finchley, I must have been a refreshing change for the admissions office. I was a bright unassuming novice who wanted to attend Harvard for the right reasons and into the bargain was African born!

My father greeted the news of my admission in somewhat of the same fashion as my schoolmaster Sammy Hewson. "Why would you want to leave England for some American university in the backwaters of Boston masquerading as a pseudo

Harvard

Cambridge?" Imbued with the mythical colonial virtues of Oxbridge as the pantheon for education, he could not fathom my motives nor comprehend the possibilities that Harvard offered for his son. I was naturally disappointed with his reaction and was expecting congratulations for my initiative and plucky achievement. Thankfully, a relative, Professor Ekpechi, was familiar with Harvard and was able to persuade my father that it was indeed a worthy academic institution for his son to attend. He also explained that in some circles Harvard was even whispered to eclipse both Oxford and Cambridge combined, although admittedly not with the same historic pedigree. Professor Ekpechi was so impressed with my achievement that he wrote me a congratulatory check for one hundred U.S. dollars. "Well done! "Take this", he said smiling as he handed me the check. This was a princely sum for a London teenager then and it was the first ever sum of money I was to receive in U.S. dollars.

Having forsaken family and friends in England for adventure and some measure of ambition, I arrived at Boston's Logan Airport full of adrenalin in August 1979, with a small suitcase and trunk and was picked up by Mrs. Miller; my Harvard appointed international student host family to help with my transition to American culture and life. She was a kindly middle-aged widow who, during the short drive to her home proceeded to tell me about her only son, a college student who was shot dead while driving cabs to make ends meet one summer in South Boston. There was understandably a dark gloom in her otherwise kindly countenance. Her sadness contrasted with my giddy excitement of setting foot in America for the first time! I knew bugger all about America, but I knew enough to know pretty much straightaway that this living arrangement was not going to be a good match for me. Mrs. Miller needed time to grieve for her lost son. After several nights at Mrs. Miller's, I was keen to move into my Holworthy Hall dorms in Harvard Yard to start dorm crew cleaning bathrooms on campus which I had been reliably assured by the office for foreign students was a great way to make friends ahead of freshman week and to acclimatize to the hard working ethos of Americans. My first challenging encounter was with a soda machine. Thirsty after my dorm crew excursions in Cambridge's sweltering, humid summer, I stood face-to-face with a soda machine offering Coca Cola, (as I would later discover) vile tasting Dr. Pepper, Pepsi, 7-Up, Root Beer, TAB and various other assorted diet and/or low calorie sodas. The machines I knew in England offered only Coca Cola or Pepsi and perhaps on occasion 7-Up or Fanta orange. I was overwhelmed by the choices available and stood bemused in front of the machine. A youthful, spirited, athletic and rather attractive dark haired Mediterranean looking girl behind me registered my confusion and came to my rescue. She explained in a thick Boston accent, as best she could, each of the options on offer. "This is how you operate the machine", slotting in a quarter and pressing the desired button to dispense the thirst quenching nectar I desperately needed. Her family lived in Raynham, Massachusetts and her Boston accent sounded very exotic. She in turn found mine apparently foreign and amusing but nevertheless pleasing to the ear. Her name was Ellen and we would later meet again while doing laundry and again at track practice that afternoon. Ellen and I had an innocent but intense romance our sophomore year that was to span several decades on-and-off. Beneath Ellen's outer beauty was a complex and intense inner personality. I admired her pride in her local working class roots; there was a sincere genuineness, an authenticity that made Ellen special. She was at the same time deeply analytical, fearful of trusting, and conflicted about me because of my race and her belief that I was yet another rich kid on campus. She had stumbled on the curious snare I met often in America, the mistaken belief that a well-spoken gentlemanly upbringing and bearing equated to monetary wealth. It was true my paternal grandmother was a local princess and that an uncle through marriage had been knighted by Her Britannic Majesty, The Queen of England, but we could hardly have been called Rockefellers, even by Nigerian standards. We were at the time comfortable rather than hugely wealthy. The label of aristo-cachet was hard nevertheless to shake. It was unclear to me, and I suspect to Ellen too, how we could bridge the cultural perception gap between us, which looked at times like a treacherous field of broken glass. I was far from the young man whom I suspected she imagined herself falling in love with and bringing home to meet her family. For my part, I was clueless about my ideal soul mate. This unwittingly may have been part of my attraction for Ellen. I had no sense of the barriers that regiment social relations in America. I defied the norm. This may have been interpreted as refreshing in the American context where people are quickly compartmentalized: Asian, black, white, Catholic, Jewish...WASP. There seemed to be no clear middle ground for Ellen and me. We had a beautiful innocent love at a time when we both were still searching for our own identities. This made our break-up very painful. We were ill equipped at that formative juncture to build on strengths in our friendship; to move from banal sophomoric romance to the intimacy that would make for a lasting union together. I remember planning for us to visit my roommate's host family in Dorchester for a dinner. Ellen arrived at my dorm wearing bright red pants, a color which in Nigeria was considered less than flattering unless one was prowling the streets at night. The outfit in hindsight was flattering and fitted her beautiful Middle Eastern complexion and strong personality, but the look on my face when she arrived for the date said otherwise. We quarreled and Ellen soon left for tranquil peace in her dorm room. I did not know where to begin to explain myself and how to expunge thoughts drilled into pathways in my mind that logically had no basis in the circumstances I was in. Ellen did not take kindly to my explanation, which she understandably found offensive and hurtful. We had not yet decoded our complex cultural histories, which guided how we responded to each other and those around us. Her mother, who I heard much about, but never met, was of Lebanese decent and her father who survived remarkable depravation and adversity in his own American journey, now late, was Irish. Together they raised eight children. Ellen and I shared the common attributes of straddling cultures, being from large families, having humanist leanings, and enjoying running and healthy sporting pursuits. Ellen also had a "wicked" sense of (flippant) humor and liked to drink tea, which was a big plus for me. We stayed and remain friends; periodically challenging and pushing each other to do our best in life.

    I had some surprising linguistic challenges in my first few weeks at Harvard having arrived assuming that Britain and America shared a common language. My first blunder was at a reception freshman week where I complimented a female classmate: "You have a homely comportment". This was met with an astonished, if-looks-could-kill icy stare. She marched off in the opposite direction clearly annoyed at my flattering remarks. Upon enquiring further from my roommates if this was a customary way of parting in America; there was a collective shudder. "You said what to her face?" From all accounts my innocent comments were less than flattering in America. Homely I quickly learnt meant ugly and unattractive in American-English, the correct word in American-English it would appear was homey which although slightly better was not necessarily regarded as a positive attribute by some of my Harvard-Radcliffe peers. Despite my overall exuberance, I had a sense at times of walking on eggshells, linguistic dangers and subtle cultural nuances lurked at every turn.

My freshman roommates and I shared two adjoining suites with a common bathroom in-between. We were in the last all male entrance on the Freshman Yard, which made for a testosterone filled freshman year devoid of the leveling female influence we would have greatly benefited from. In my suite was Bruce a talented Glee Club singer and ski jumper from New Hampshire who I shared bunks with. Bruce confided in me one evening as we lay in our respective bunk beds, "Gus I'm Gay". This was hardly a surprise to me having met Bruce's circle of campus friends and acquaintances. It was nevertheless a delicate and sensitive subject. I told Bruce "it frankly makes no odds to me; I would never think less of you or indeed anyone else because they are different". He was uncertain how our vocal roommates might react in a post-Village People era. It was to be a painful year for Bruce; he eventually came-out toward the end of freshman year, navigated dealing with his family and a young woman from New Hampshire who seemed extremely keen on him. I had a great deal of respect and empathy for Bruce since I knew how he felt to be excluded for stupid prejudices. Our roommates for the most part were supportive although not without some muscular youthful bravado. Bruce shared with me some of his relief and feeling of freedom once he finally came-out, and the joy and excitement of journeying to New York, the Mecca for east coast gays.

I rejected all invitations to join Harvard's illustrious undergraduate private dining clubs called Finals Clubs, including the patrician Porcellian, in protest because one of my freshman roommates who was Jewish, women, and other minorities were being excluded by some clubs. The vestiges of disdainful practices still haunted the hallowed halls of Harvard. It was clear that at Harvard there were those for whom the college fit like a glove, i.e., without the sometimes-awkward cultural transition presented for me as a foreign student of color new to Harvard and America. These were students who knew America and its institutions. Their ranks included Mayflower decedents whose families had attended Harvard over many generations and prep school scholars, as well as sons and daughters of the rich, famous, and infamous. In contrast, I always had to explain myself and who I was. Some classmates refused to believe there were black people living in England and were convinced my accent was somehow mysteriously acquired; they clearly would have been more comfortable if I said I was from the South Bronx or Harlem. Others assumed I was the son of a rich oil magnate or a deposed African dictator. There were also a good many nice down-to-earth students who seemed to accept me for who I was, a teenager with a strange accent, eager to learn, eat pizza (with my hands and not with a knife and fork as we did in England) and to have fun.

Having been on dorm crew I was the first to arrive in our rooms and was greeted by a dirty smelly individual who waltzed into the room and declared with an effusive smirk "Hello", I'm your neighbor from the adjoining suite". Bharat had just returned from a pre-Harvard wilderness expedition where they were caught in a major squall. We became fast and close friends and shared many adventures. We delighted in telling some of our fellow students who were not too good on geography or accents: "Pleased to meet you!" delivered in a measured deliberate received-BBC (English) accent. "This is my roommate Bharat." "He is from Broken Knuckles Wisconsin and I am from Rutland Vermont". These were both parts of the United States not known for their population of color. The students readily accepted our explanation although some did harbor a lingering doubt on their faces. I roomed with Bharat for my remaining years as an upper classman in Claverly Hall (affiliated to Quincy House), a regal annex adjacent from the Harvard Lampoon castle. The gold leaf wallpapered rooms once housed the Vanderbilt offspring. For me it was the lap of luxury, the likes of which I would not experience again until many years of arduous labor in New York. My wonderment at Harvard was like that I encountered when I first arrived in England. I was amazed by the university's extraordinary facilities and the array of activities available to students to pursue, from sports to theater and drama. Nothing was spared in the pursuit of knowledge.

Bharat came to Harvard from India having attended Atlantic College in Llantwit Major in the Vale of Glamorgan Wales in the United Kingdom. A Calcutta native and product of the elite Doon School and St. Stephens College in Delhi, he caused endless amusement by telling our unsuspecting roommates that he started his day after yoga in India putting out milk for the local snakes. A tale some of our roommates were not altogether sure was true or false.

This ambiguity which we fostered and sometimes played-off annoyed and irritated our All-American roommates and was a cause of some tension. In any event, Bharat was a gifted musician and played the sitar. I therefore had the good fortune to be put to sleep most nights by serene midnight ragas except for the six weeks he invited his mother during finals and my general exams in the Government department to share our cramped dorm room. Many visiting guests shared our confined quarters and regularly slept on our floor in sleeping bags, including a bright and jovial young friend of Bharat's, now sadly deceased, who went on to become a famed and storied senior executive at eBay. Occasionally he would give concerts at other Houses or for the International Students Association. He even kindly tried to teach me how to play the sitar and surbahar its larger cousin. Unfortunately, I lacked a musical ear and the suppleness to assume the contorted yoga sitting position required to master both instruments; my soccer playing thighs were simply too big for me to be a sitar player.

    One winter morning after a heavy snowstorm, while on the way back from breakfast, I met my roommates eagerly in discussion about a beach party they were planning in our rooms that evening. They were discussing the logistics for moving out furniture and how to spirit-in buckets of sand under the superintendent's nose to fill the room from a construction site at the Gulf gas station by the Freshman Union where we all ate. I thought this was one of their many crazy American schemes that would come to naught, but I returned later that evening to hear music and flashing strobe lights from our fourth floor dorms with drunken swimming trunks and bikini clad students tumbling down the stairs. Yankee ingenuity, which I would grow over the years to respect and admire, had won; they had indeed filled the living room of our dorm with ankle deep sand. Flush with their success, my roommates were not shy to remind me "This is America [where anything is possible], love it or leave it Mofo!" The next morning my roommates, once more or less sober, swept the sand down the stairs and out the front door into a huge mound in The Yard. The Superintendent was livid, incensed by the bald-faced cheek of my roommates. Our Supervisor was equally ticked-off and used some choice words in the presence of our innocent ears. This episode placed my roommates in folklore legend among party aficionados at Harvard. The beach party idea was brilliantly conceived and executed. We duly inscribed all our names outside our window in the historic bricks around the windows of our Holworthy dorms along with those from past generations.

For good measure, we also received a dressing-down from our genial and sporting Turkish Proctor, Hasan Kayali. Hasan was an alumnus of the Harvard track mafia of horizontal jumpers. He was an attendee of the Mifundi Table, which met regularly at the Spanish Restaurant Iruna, where squid in ink sauce, and callos (tripe) was consumed with copious quantities of white and red sangria, collegially quaffed amid lively jocular repast. The table was named after a singularly unique incident whereas legend has it; Sola Mahoney a tall striking athletic blue-black Gambian with Nigerian-Yoruba heritage was repeatedly pushed aside as he stepped forward at the Hilltops restaurant in Braintree, Massachusetts each time the maître d'hôtel called-out, "table ready for the Mahoney party". On his next visit to forestall embarrassment he booked a table under the satirical and very unassuming nom de guerre of Kingston Mifundi. There were no problems with his table on that night. Race in America rears its head in the strangest of places. The Mifundi Table had more than a splash of color about it, which gave the uninformed impression to some that it was only for those of color. This misapprehension was soon dispelled as Messrs.' Boyd, Hall, O'Brien, and Sellers became not infrequent attendees. None, I might add, where consumed by the squid and sangria loving cannibals, nor emerged with their heads shrunken on a pole. On the contrary, even non-jumpers of all colors, religions, and persuasions, were now quick to accept invitations to our hallowed table.

Bharat would talk me into all sorts of escapades including going to visit a hermit friend of his in the frozen wilds of Canada in the middle of winter the Christmas of our freshman year. The hermit's name was Jean Juneau and Bharat's parents apparently had met him while on holiday in San Tropez! We bought airline tickets for about $29 round trip; we had to go back to Crimson Travel to check they had not undercharged. Ominously they confirmed that the fare was correct; not a popular tourist destination in the middle of winter. Undeterred, we flew to Montreal where the hermit's sister picked us up and drove us into the wilderness to the cabin with a potbelly stove on the shore of Lac des Deux Montagnes. We spent about a week living and sleeping in the cabin, ice fishing for nourishment (supplemented by canned goods), not bathing, and pissing in a can, we threw the waste out the window and it froze before it hit the ground! I even tried my hand one day at downhill skiing to keep warm. We wore layers upon layers of pullovers underneath our heavy coats newly purchased from the winter sales at Filene's Basement. Jean warned that if we left our extremities exposed for more than a few minutes we would lose our appendages to frostbite. We philosophized at night with the hermit about "oneness" and on New Year's Eve we donned tennis rackets on our feet (snow shoes) to go to his neighbor's house some five or so miles away. Jean left us trailing in the neck deep snow walking like a man half his age. Behind us we could see his cabin silhouetted against the lake, the sun blinding, reflecting off the frozen snow covered lake as the wind chill whistled by at well below minus 32 degrees Fahrenheit. Our host was a charming, slightly balding, graying, willowy French Canadian man and his younger attractive English spouse and young son. Bharat and I were relieved and dizzy with joy to be in the warmth and comfort of a sumptuous and beautiful cabin which felt like heaven after days sleeping in the crawl space above Jean's cabin covered with smelly smoke filled blankets and pelts. There was electricity and running water and a flushing toilet! The husband, Gilles, played the piano and we sang and drank merrily all through the night before trudging back home to the cabin, fearful of hungry bears. At the end of our stay we were picked up once again by his sister and we went to stay with college friends in the posh Mont-Royal area in Montreal. When we rang the doorbell our friend's mother shrieked and called-out for her husband saying, "There are a pair of dodgy looking filthy bums at the door". We managed, finally to explain who we were and were allowed in the house on the condition that we should bathe and shave immediately. We told them about the hermit and how we had complimented Gilles on his singing upon which he presented us with two of his own LPs. Their faces lit-up with excitement and in unison they shouted, "How could you have been in the company of Gilles Vigneault the legendary iconoclast French Canadian folk lyricist without even asking for his autograph on the LPs?" We had goofed once again.

In our freshman year Bharat persuaded nearly all our rooming group to venture with him to a mixer at the all-girls Wellesley College. On arrival we discovered his mission, to woo and win the charms of the beautiful Jashri, fortified with the Dutch courage of a man with his posse at his side. Realizing our "B" roles in Bharat's movie we turned tail back on the very next bus to Harvard Square leaving Bharat with a Cheshire cat grin once again.

I had many good and some terrible instructors at Harvard, my favorites were Elliot Cohen who supervised my Government seminars and walked me through the Lincoln-Douglas Debates, the captivating Democracy in America by Alexis de Tocqueville and the political history of America. We had some lively debates reminiscent of those of my secondary schoolmate Sylvester on Elliot's right-wing views on engagement with South Africa. I had participated in various protests to prompt Harvard to divest and was not amused by his engagement theories. He however did instill in me the values of rigorous analytical thought reinforced by the infamous Harvey (C minus) Mansfield the philosopher famed for single handedly defending grade inflation at Harvard, whose course I also took.

I returned to England the summer after my freshman year at Harvard to compete at the Amateur Athletics Association (AAA) Championships, which was the UK's national championship and placed second with a leap of 7.64 meters in the long jump competition. I led until the final round before surrendering victory to the reigning (Montreal) Olympic Champion, Arnie Robinson, in front a packed stadium of 15,000 spectators at Crystal Palace on a perfectly sunny, cool and still day. I remember being taken aback by the sound of the crowd's spontaneous applause and rising from the sandpit looking up stunned to discover they were actually applauding me. On another less auspicious day, I was featured on Grandstand, the BBC's prime time sports show. "Gus Udo the precocious up-and-coming star from Shaftesbury Harriers is leading coming off the bend in his first major 200 meter race". Only to be overtaken like a speeding express train in the home straight by almost the entire field. I was drafted into the race at the last moment for my club Shaftesbury Harriers persuaded by our energetic team manager and guiding light, Geoff Morphitis, not knowing I would be humiliated on national television at prime viewing time. Allen Wells gold medalist at 100 meters and silver medalist in the 200 meters at the Moscow Olympics won the race. Suffice it to say that I did not terribly enjoy my twenty-two fleeting seconds of fame. It did however provide countless mirth for an untold number of friends, family, and acquaintances. As my close friend and Harvard track colleague Jim Johnson put it, "You should have made it twenty-seconds of fame".

Each spring a select group from the track team would venture on a trip to a sunny location for warm weather training. In my freshman year we went to Troy State Alabama, which was a bit of a shock considering the team journeyed to Puerto Rico the year before. The locals were still coming to terms with the end of segregation. This seemed much in evidence on the campus and made the ethnically mixed team very uncomfortable, particularly members of color like me. I struck up conversation with a delicate young woman near the college's library, which appeared to be used sparingly by students. She was a beauty pageant winner from Vermont on scholarship! Clearly talented, she cautioned, "This is not like the North", "stay away from fraternity parties", and in a hushed kindly concerned tone, "you would be wise to follow unspoken color bars here". The track itself was rock hard, so much so that we could not workout on it more than once a day. The weather, cold, wet and raining was less than optimal for the intended purpose of the trip; warm weather training! I hoped at least that the college had gotten a very favorable discount on our food and lodgings. For most of our time there the entire team was wet and miserable. We were ill prepared for the unseasonably inclement weather dress wise since we had all expected glorious sunshine. The next year we went to Florida State University, which was a big improvement and then to Louisiana State University, and finally to Houston, Texas in our senior year. My roommate during most of these trips was my co-jumper Jim Johnson, with whom I joked, (especially about the boat-like size 14 galoshes that he docked next to my locker on snowy days), and practiced most days. Jim, a shrewd and extremely sharp New Jersey native was instrumental in helping me decipher and navigate America-speak and culture. He had a remarkable sensitivity for the foibles of his countrymen and women of all races and creeds. He understood the history of Americans in all their shapes and sizes, their baggage, prejudices, strengths, and aspirations. Tackling and understanding unspoken WASP culture of entitlement that oozed from the pores of some of my colleagues and the complex race dynamics and power politics on campus was not an easy task for a new arrival on America's shores. Each college-dining hall featured tables, isolated islands, which drew various groups, e.g., blacks,

Asians, gays and other minorities seeking to focus attention on their needs. These shows of solidarity, like the country's political system, seemed to function as healthy checks and balances against tyranny of the majority. Sometimes they were misread, in my view, as a threat or retreat into a ghetto. This was a new phenomenon for me and very different from the U.K. philosophy of blending in every way except for the obvious, one's color, which could be "discounted" by the English if all other boxes were ticked-off (checked). Once accepted, differences notwithstanding, you were part of the "Club".

We also journeyed to England and Ireland that year to compete in the bi-annual Harvard-Yale Oxford-Cambridge meet, which we won handily. As co-captain, I delivered a speech at the banquet dinner, which seemed to cause some degree of mirth in the audience. I borrowed from Ibo proverbs to thank our hosts for permitting us to drink from their river. Thereafter we adjourned to the Spade and Becket pub on the banks of the River Cam to resume our transatlantic détente. Regrettably, I could not contain my unbridled enthusiasm on the trip. Against the wise counsel of our ambassadorial Swedish trainer and new Head Coach, Frank Haggerty; both of whom knew my history of injury in the event, I participated in the high jump. I slipped a disc clearing for about the twentieth time 2.00 meters or a shade less than 6 feet 7 inches; a psychological ceiling I was unable to break. The back injury left me prone and effectively ended my track career in what was my final meet for Harvard. It was a great disappointment and shame since I was in the best shape of my sporting life. I jumped a few more times that summer for my Club but my back was and has never been the same since.

I also never broke Harvard's oldest track record, which was in the long jump. The record is by Olympian Ned Gourdin who leapt 25 feet 3 inches or 7.70 meters. I believe the record still stands today. Entering Harvard after recovering my freshman year from a badly mangled foot, sustained while high jumping against the advice of my U.K. coach, I was convinced that I would break the record. The infamous technical coaching of the helpless and harmless Edgar B. Stowell, "Use your arms...well okay, go higher" did not help much and nor did the myriad of excellent intellectually stimulating campus distractions offered in-and-out of class. I quickly learnt from running track that time was our enemy and that timely disciplined execution was critical to reach one's potential, it was not enough to know you could, succeeding in crystallizing a goal was so much more powerful and intoxicating.

My best jump of 7.64 meters as a sophomore was at the AAAs, an out of college meet. I did produce a prodigious unrecorded leap my senior year at the Ivy League's Heptagonal Championships which undoubtedly eclipsed Gourdin's record mark. It was however nullified by the track official as a foul; having been marginally beyond the takeoff board. For my part, I could not see any telltale spike marks in the Plasticine immediately beyond the takeoff board, to indicate it was indeed a foul, although admittedly I did not have my spectacles on. I was in good form and confident I could repeat or surpass the mark. The omens were not good that day at Cornell; the weather turned in minutes from glorious sunshine to freezing driving snow, negating any opportunities to repeat my first jump. The opportunity was lost forever despite my unbridled optimism. Our team did however win the meet. We were Outdoor and Indoor Heptagonal

Harvard

Champions. This double accomplishment was a testament not only to the athletic talent of the team but the leadership and discipline, which I helped, bring to the team as co-captain. Regrettably, some might say laughably, I am still waiting to be inducted into Harvard Track's Hall of Fame. I am not losing any sleep, like the Finals Clubs of yonder year; it may be best avoided for me.

My romantic life took some sharp lefts-and-rights. After Ellen, I met a very sweet and beautiful young woman whose mother was Cuban and father was Australian. She was a year ahead of me but decades ahead in terms of planning our lives together. Brilliant, she had been admitted into both Harvard and Yale law school; she elected to go to the latter. I sadly did not share her conviction about the future path of our relationship and we broke up shortly before the end of my junior year. I was her first real love and it was unfortunate we did not meet later in my life when I had caught up with her plans for us. I then dated another very smart young lady from South Carolina named Jackie, who combined her intellect with a very curvaceous form. Jackie was an exotic mix of Native and Black American and I fell rather badly for her charms. She captured my heart by leaving a single red rose in front of my door after a late night library stint. Our relationship would end calamitously after I left her that summer to return to London to see my family. On returning to college that fall her roommate informed me she had had a breakdown of sorts and was now dating a female lecturer at the college. We had spent a blissful week in Martha's Vineyard together before my departure for London, I was crushed. Complicated matters of the heart such as these were unfamiliar to me. My road to recovery was not an easy one. I was concurrently dealing with unexpected and unannounced news that my father had taken a third wife. This was not a matter easily shared or understood by roommates and faculty alike. These were unique emotional experiences that at times left me isolated on campus since there were relatively few other African students to share my pain with. Father had elected once again not to inform us until after the deed was done. Like Henry VIII, he defended his traditional Onitsha matrimonial rights. "I will marry who I want, when I want." "I don't need permission from you or anyone else". Worse still he was continuing to face business challenges and exchange control difficulties remitting my college fees. I was compelled to take on a loan from the university.

All this unhappiness and uncertainty coincided with the pressures of upcoming graduation. To make matters worse I failed a pass-fail course "The Picaresque in Spanish Literature" which I had no business taking, especially with a professor who failed students for missing the occasional lecture. I wrote a paper that summer to complete my Harvard degree and resolved not to repeat the mistake at the London School of Economics and Political Science (LSE) where I had been admitted for graduate school ahead of graduation. Mercifully I did extremely well in my departmental generals in the Government department and submitted a thesis; my other grades, As and some Bs, were also sufficient to satisfy the LSE admissions committee and my LSE don.

This was not the ideal movie ending I had hoped to my otherwise illustrious Harvard career. There was, indeed, no America without tears. It was a bittersweet end to my romance with Harvard and America. It also was not an easy thing to explain to proud parents who had travelled across the Atlantic for their son's graduation. I was again reminded about the

Harvard

vicissitudes and randomness of misfortune in life. Fortunately, I still had my degree, support of family, friends, and prospects of attending the LSE to look forward to. I had been spared the fate of Dustin Hoffman in the Graduate; reduced to loitering at home and being an awkward piece of furniture for embarrassed and disappointed parents to explain to visiting guests.

13. London School of Economics and Political Science (LSE)

In the back seat of a cab speeding down Storrow Drive, heading to Logan Airport for my Pan Am flight destined for London, I wondered if I would ever return to America. I was leaving behind the country's inspirational "can-do" culture, which imbued confidence to those, fortunate enough to reach her shores. I was parting Cambridge with precious cargo, know-how about the New World and my place in the world. After four years at Harvard, I had overcome many of the assimilation travails that dogged my formative years in England. I was sad too because of the many good friends I might not see again. My return to England was soon to reinforce the depth of my attachment to America and American ways of thinking and doing things. I was eager however to hear my mother's customary cheerful refrain following any long journey, Nno ije! (Welcome home!).

Not having a campus and nestled in the heart of London near Fleet Street, the former epicenter of the world of journalism, the LSE was very different from Harvard. It was a truly international university where most of the students were post-graduates from around the globe. It also had a varied and deep foreign faculty, which made for many points of view on most subjects. Students were true citizens of the world. I fitted like a glove and was as excited at being admitted to the LSE, as I was to have gained admittance to Harvard. The LSE was my dream before the opportunity to attend Harvard came along. I gladly accepted the LSE's offer thinking I was joining the ranks of the Fleet Street marching radical and expressive new thinking students I had long admired. The LSE students of those years were long gone but

London School of Economics and Political Science (LSE)

this did not stop me from having a wonderful academic and social experience at the school.

I described my time at the LSE at an alumnus breakfast with Sir Howard Davis, the School's Director at New York's Four Seasons Hotel, as the best year of my life, unparalleled other than by the birth of my children. My fellow students in my department were two lively and jovial Canadians, two male German doctorate students, a very bright English civil servant who was a part-time student, and a lovely Scottish young woman. Despite our diversity, we were a close academic unit and spent sessions after our evening seminars with our tutor in the pub below Lincolns Chamber debating the ins-and-outs of contemporary African politics and government, particularly unfolding events in turbulent Zimbabwe and South Africa.

I shared a flat in Belsize Park rented from a schoolteacher who offered rooms to young professionals like my flat-mate and me. An equally youthful English stockbroker trainee who from what I could tell spent most of his time outside work drinking excessively with his colleagues. Most nights he arrived home singing out-of-tune, inebriated stumbling up the narrow stairs to the attic, which housed our two rooms. We were permitted to use the kitchen when our landlord was not around and the toilet and bathroom. The living room though was strictly off limits being John's exclusive preserve. The house owner claimed that Hastings Banda the founder of Malawi had lived in the building as a student. He did permit me its use once when he was away for the weekend for a small drinks party, which was ruined when the owner of the house who lived across the road saw young female students entering the house, and let himself in to barge-in on the party. The presence of a lanky dirty old man did not go down well.

OYIBOS

Unfortunately I could hardly throw him out as the owner of the house, although I desperately wanted to. The guests soon took their leave followed by the house owner after he had had his fill of drinks.

What made the time special was not my accommodation but being in a familiar place, the city of my youth. I was near my family, my mother, brothers and sisters, all of whom I missed terribly while in Cambridge. I also missed the company of old school buddies from Finchley and newly acquired friends from Harvard who I got to know much better outside of the surreal confines of Cambridge. I enjoyed activities like attending London's West End theatre at student rates, outdoor concerts on Hampstead Heath by the lake, and watching new up-and-coming bands like Ian Drury and the Blockheads and Elvis Costello at local pubs. I was also studying what I loved. I journeyed occasionally to Cambridge at the invitation of the younger brother of a college track friend to enjoy civilized conversation, dinner, and port from the historic cellars at Emmanuel College, Cambridge. I missed America too and stayed in regular letter correspondence with a few close friends.

During my year at the LSE, I had the opportunity to visit Nigeria on my holidays and witnessed first-hand at least one coup in 1983, when the country's second civilian government was overthrown. I was on holiday when I noticed tanks filling-up from the nearby barracks at the local gas (petrol) station the night before the coup. We woke to martial music on the radio and television. The coup announcement played repeatedly, and was made ominously from the army's Dodon Barracks fortress by Brigadier Sani Abacha, a future dictator in the making. A dawn to dusk curfew was ordered and a series of comical incidents ensued.

London School of Economics and Political Science (LSE)

A state governor arriving excitedly back from a foreign shopping spree funded by government coffers, rushed to his home state radio station to denounce "false" coup rumors. On arrival at the local radio station, the military coup plotters promptly arrested him. One well-known politician usually seen cruising around in a Rolls Royce, disguised himself as a priest and was apprehended driving a VW Beetle while trying to head for the nearest border crossing. Others cross-dressed as women fled forgetting to shave their beards and mustaches. There was little if any real bloodshed from gunfire. Most of the injuries seemed to be from bruised egos and politicians contemplating time in the country's rat infested jails. The experience, as comical as it was, I suspect colored my decision not to return to Nigeria permanently.

On finishing the LSE, I ended up applying for over one hundred jobs and training positions in the United Kingdom. My friends were astonished at the remarkable number first and second interviews I was invited to by leading investment banks, consulting firms, commodities trading firms, and oil companies, names like: Cargill, Goldman Sachs, McKinsey, Nikko Securities, and Shell to name a few. There were over 50 interviews, but none yielded a single offer! Yes, I had the privilege of being rejected by the City's best. Was it my choice of tie or my shoes? By comparison, many of my "local" peers were lucky to obtain even a handful of interviews but most without exception found a good position within three to six months of graduating. My genius econometrician friend Jonathan, who was from the East End of London and was of Caribbean heritage, had a similar experience. He elected to pursue further education at Cambridge where he lectured and later at Imperial College before accepting a Commonwealth Scholarship to complete his doctorate at Queen's University in Canada. He then returned to take up a position with "The Old Lady of Threadneedle Street", the metonym for the Bank of England and until recently worked for a major U.K. hedge fund before founding his own research firm. A circuitous route but it was one of the few available for black students like us to gain entry into the City. Mainstream City firms were clearly not ready to take a chance on recruits of color in any numbers. The thought did occur to me that perhaps I was not qualified until I looked at those who were being offered positions and their qualifications and experience relative to mine. Frustrated, at the advice of various friends in New York I switched my focus from the City of London to Wall Street and within a few short weeks I was offered a position at Shearson Lehman Brothers. I completed the obligatory battery of obnoxious interviews with various firms, where questions were asked about my zealous commitment to forsaking family, friends, sleep, and reason for the investment-banking cult of making money. The perennial favorite question was: "where do you see yourself in three or five years' time". The answer to me was obvious: "not in investment banking", but such a response was unlikely to be understood by my interlocutors; followers of the modern money sect, who saw little else beyond the windows and walls of the firm. It was Lehman that provided the coveted job offer, as it would happen, even before formally receiving my resume. From all accounts all my Harvard peers at Lehman spoke well of my character and that was sufficient for the firm. This, I later learned to my benefit, was deemed exceedingly unusual and a favorable omen.

14. Love and Lehman

Having made the vast cultural journey from Shackleford Street, Lagos to Wall Street, the absence of a moral basis for acquiring wealth was deeply troubling to me during my early period of training at Shearson Lehman Brothers. Imbued with Catholic accented traditional Onitsha values of right and wrong, I could not come to terms with the prospect of recycling the same product without innovation to many clients at outrageous prices bearing no relationship to their cost and in the process trammeling roughshod over my peers and customers alike in search of steroid-fueled profits. Such wealth garnered immorally I was taught neither gains reward nor earns respect. I realized very early in my career that I was not going to be a mainstream Wall Street banker ready to kill my mother and to eat my children for the next buck. I had failed to complete my cultural metamorphosis into an über-Banker for whom profit was paramount. Wall Street values were at odds with my ethical roots; Lehman brought these challenges and tensions into sharp relief.

My African history professor at Harvard, Bill Freund had looked at me somewhat askance when I mentioned investment banking as a possible career choice, this should have been warning enough. Even then Wall Street was already famed for greed and excess which has only gotten worse with the passage of time.

When I arrived at Shearson Lehman in 1985, morale was low. It was following the firm's acquisition by American Express after a fierce and bitter internal struggle between trader Lewis Glucksman and the patrician investment banker Pete Peterson ex-Chairman of the Blackstone Group. Such was the resentment against the resultant acquisition that some stalwart managing directors, behaving like brooding immature school children, routinely tore down the utilitarian plastic blue-box Amex logo placed on the walls next to the elevator on each floor besides the stately Shearson Lehman name in brass.

Analysts like me, still crunched numbers on large spread sheets which limited the number of scenarios we could simulate for any transaction and greatly magnified the hours it took me and others to accurately perform this painstaking work. The advent of the personal computer (PC) caused excitement and confusion at the firm as well as the occasional fistfight as managing directors struggled to assign time to the single PC allotted each group. Management finally came to its senses and recognized the importance computers would play in the future of the financial industry. Overnight like magic every employee of merit from secretaries up had a computer at their desk. I gazed proudly at mine each morning until I was shown how to switch it on. We were left largely to our own devises to master the intricacies of these early-complicated abacuses. A fledgling information technology (IT) department was established and staffed with prerequisite geeks. It was nevertheless evident that for some of the older managing directors computers would not replace the abacus and side-rule residing in their drawers. To them IBM's miraculous technology in a box was at best an oversized corporate trophy or desk toy destined to gather dust. The dinosaurs were put out to grass one-by-one, replaced by freshly minted eager MBA's keen to move up the money chain. These MBAs served as cannon fodder for the industry, providing huge leverage for able-managing directors. Before the arrival of PCs our lives were dependent on good relationships with the characters, aspiring actors, actresses and male models that ran the Wang typing pool who if you ticked-them-off could make life for you very miserable and your day exceedingly long. Research on companies for comparables was equally tedious, dependent on millions of microfiches stored in a haphazard library with old clonking Xerox machines spitting out pages at a rate that seemed like one every few minutes. Market information was piped in by way of a primitive Quotron machine, a terminal with a dumb green and black screen, a far cry from today's nifty sophisticated Bloomberg or Reuter's machines. Although we worked sixty or more hours each week and earned in effect less than minimum wage we learned a great deal but also sacrificed our personal lives and time with friends and family. My college roommate recounts coming to visit to find me at the office late into the night on Christmas Eve on an assignment. Young and impressionable, we were coddled to maintain the veneer that we were masters of the universe; allowed to order surf-and-turf dinners at the office after eight o'clock in the evening and to take limousines home, which added to the impression we were doing something frightfully important and useful. It mattered not that often you could have been home by subway by the time the shiny black limousine actually arrived, such was the frenzied demand among other firms located downtown. Occasionally, an analyst would crack and would quit or take a leave of absence. It was not unheard of for managing directors not yet forty years old to have heart attacks at their desks; we took ourselves all too seriously. Some hapless analysts even routinely slept under their desks; one bereft of female companionship took to picking-up female limousine drivers for dates. I knew this was not the life my ancestors had chosen for me. There had to be another more pleasant way to make a living.

I was invited to an Upper West Side literary intern party by one of my analyst colleagues and it was there that I met the beautiful Daphne with her live wire fast-talking and busty roommate with big red hair. Daphne took my breath away on first sight, a statuesque strawberry blond with intelligent intense eyes and an elegant, shapely figure. I made an attempt at small talk with her lively gin quaffing siren actress (waitress) friend but was elated when Daphne actually looked my way and rescued me from my desperate attempt to make conversation. It was love at first sight for me and I hoped for her too. Although I was a slightly younger man, she agreed to go on a date and returning one evening from a romantic dinner in the West Village, where coincidentally she also lived, the skies opened with a heavy downpour, we embraced, kissed and ended up making passionate love at her apartment with the heavy rain falling outside. I walked home in the clouds euphoric; Cupid had shot me. Prior to meeting Daphne, I saw little of New York, my days were mostly spent either at the office cramped over a computer, traveling on business, or sleeping. The latter, sleep, not as much as my body craved and required for sound health. Meeting Daphne finally confirmed that it was my job that I hated, not New York. Dating in New York seemed far less complicated. There were no endless rounds of intimate dinner parties where guests were painstakingly selected in the hope of matching couples. Nor were there the matchmaking intrigues of family scrutiny that proceeded approved unsupervised dating among Onitsha families.

Daphne, a divorcee, was much more interesting to be with than the air-headed New York women I had previously met. We had great fun together. We watched her roommate's boyfriend's band, The Rumprollers performing sets at the Nancy Whiskey Pub downtown on Lispenard Street in Tribeca, attended readings of both new and prominent writers, saw off off Broadway plays at Circle Rep and came home tipsy to slow dance to UB40's "I Got You Babe". We were young and in love and I was Daphne's superman, her hero, as she wrote in a touching Valentine card.

Within a few months of meeting, we were living together in my one-bedroom walk-up brownstone apartment on the Upper West Side much to the annoyance of the host of the party where Daphne and I met since it was she that I was supposed to be asking out. I had inherited the new apartment from the girlfriend of my extremely nice landlord-roommate, the son of Jeb McGruder of Watergate fame, when he and his girlfriend moved out of New York to attend their respective business schools.   My time with Daphne was some of my happiest but eight months into our romance things began to take a turn for the worse. I was struggling to come to terms with what to do once my analyst internship came to an end. My choices were either Business School or returning to London. Business school was not a real option given that my father's business was floundering and that exchange controls were getting tighter and tighter and student loans were out of the question since I was not a U.S. passport holder. All this could have been resolved if I had married Daphne but this was not the foundation on which I wanted to start a lifelong relationship. For Daphne, marriage was the right solution. And pigheadedness, as she saw it, drove her to distraction and despair. Daphne had already met my family in London and was roundly approved by all, with the exception of my father who had not met her.

My friends also liked her very much and many thought she was a great catch for me.

Daphne was working for a well-known New York literary agent and was building, with my encouragement and support, a solid career in the field. She offered to support me in turn while I found my feet but did not want to move to London because of her career. Pride would not permit me to take up her kind loving offer; matters were made worse for me by the tensions that surfaced once her father discovered that I was not Italian like her elder sister's boyfriend but was actually a young man of color from Africa. Her father unleashed a torrent of verbal abuse on his daughter. I asked a tearful Daphne, "What's the matter?" Thinking perhaps there had been a death in the family. She put down the receiver, her lips quivering as she explained what had happened. I in turn felt terrible for Daphne and resented being rejected by a man I had not even met or spoken to. My Onitsha impulses kicked-in; it was important for me to marry a woman whose family would accept me for who I was and not what they thought I was. It was difficult to understand how a father would treat a wonderful daughter in such a horrible unjust manner because of the color of my skin. It was not long after that Daphne moved back in with her old roommate and despite a failed attempt at reconciliation our paths unfortunately had changed forever.

My first meaningful assignment at Shearson Lehman was being selected to work for the prized Financial Institutions Group's (FIGs) analyst pool on a project for famed banker Sandy Weill who was making a bid for Bank of America. We received calls from our boss; Mary Sykes who headed the analyst program that we were to cancel all weekend plans. We thought this was a little excessive, after all what could be so important that it required all four analysts in the group, vice presidents, senior vice-presidents and managing directors on standby for an entire weekend. Weill's audacious move ultimately failed but not before me and my analyst colleagues had worked with no sleep non-stop from Friday afternoon to Monday morning when we were told to go home and shower and to return to find out the outcome of Weill's proposal later that morning in San Francisco. After we were done Mr. Weill personally came down to thank all of us and shook hands with each and every analysts on the project for our heroic work compiling a massive pitch-book which today with computers might have taken a couple of hours tops for a smart eighth grader.

Friends at work included stalwarts, like Frank Yeary, who nursed investment-banking ambitions from a tender age. From the outset, Frank was a mature competent banker compared to the rest of us; some like me were still struggling to distinguish the firm's business activities from those of the United Nations! There was no noblesse oblige on Wall Street as I would discover. Frank rose rapidly at Lehman and was soon to become the Global Co-Chairman of Mergers and Acquisitions at Citigroup having risen through the ranks at Salomon Brother before they were rescued by Warren Buffet and taken over by Citibank. Frank lived, as I did, in the West Village, in a Bohemian walk-up with a shared bathroom down the hall. We were a short commute to our collegial Water Street office, which occupied several floors in the building. The firm was so small that you knew most people by name or at least recognized their faces. It was not unusual to run into the diminutive cigar smoking Peter Cohen, the firm's CEO walking the floors or in an elevator. We were on nodding terms since I was very conspicuous; there were few professionals of color at the firm. I believe there were a managing director, a Harvard Business School professor, in investment banking and a couple of associates. The firm later moved to Vesey Street in the newly constructed World Financial Center.

One of the rare occasions I actually drove in America, having learnt to drive in England on the other-side of the road, was with Daphne for the wedding of a Harvard classmate. On this occasion I managed to crash the car, which we had borrowed from her playful sister, who I was fond of, en route to the wedding sending us spinning on the highway into headlong traffic. It all happened in a split second but like my drowning experience seemed to be in slow motion; miraculously no one was injured, we were shaken enough however not to continue to the nuptials. The wheel nuts apparently had not been sufficiently tightened after a recent tire change. Daphne's sister was furious and insisted that I pay for repairs which I did. The event left some significant dents in my relationship with Daphne who, in any event, was not a big fan of my driving.

On another project I was sent to accompany one of the managing directors to visit a bank in Grand Rapids Michigan with whom the firm apparently had a mergers and acquisitions mandate. I arrived in Grand Rapids exhausted having stayed up late for several nights trying to master the group's enormous capital model spreadsheet while simultaneously learning how to work an IBM computer. To make matters worse I had assumed that Grand Rapids was somewhere up state and a few hours train ride away. I was startled when my assistant pointed-out that unless I left immediately, "Yes immediately, now!" and travelled non-stop to Chicago connecting on a puddle-hopper to Grand Rapids I would not make the meeting. I raced out of the building flagging the first yellow cab in sight with entrails of a half completed pitch-book under my arms. On arrival I explained my confusion to the managing director who was very understanding and seemed more concerned with how he would persuade the board of the bank to throw half-a-million dollars at the firm for five minutes work by the typing pool. The bank in question had refused to pay a $500,000 fee for an acquisition they had independently completed with an institution covered in the mandate agreement. We were in-front of the board made up of sensible mid-Westerners who not unnaturally saw no reason to pay Lehman a $500,000 fee for including a target bank on a two page typed list. I am sure the matter was more complex than I am painting, but suffice it to say that despite the sincere and compelling arguments put forth by the managing director, we were tossed out of the meeting without even an offer of a glass of water or a cab to the airport. These were the days when sense and logic still prevailed in the market place. I had a great deal of sympathy and respect for our client and their refusal to be bamboozled by the firm but I kept my own counsel.

For a period I was also assigned as the young analyst on the Chase mergers and acquisition account which included periodic attendance at meetings with the bank's tall courtly Chief Executive Officer Thomas Labrecque and Chief Financial Officer a short pugnacious accountant of Italian extraction with little if any patience for clueless young subordinates. I sat at the meetings dreading the moment all eyes would suddenly turn on me and the feared question would be asked "where did this number come from?" A single figure buried deep in a book of several hundred pages of spreadsheet printouts. It was the job of the analyst unwaveringly to provide a concise, if not precise explanation. Fortunately the managing director with whom the account was entrusted was adroit at moving away from such questions before the poor analyst concerned was verbally pulverized into mincemeat right there and then in the CEO's office. Now I understood why colleagues were less than sanguine about undertaking this seemingly plum assignment. I was glad however, "Big picture", to be introduced to the workings of the financial world and to the thinking of the brilliant minds of one of the world's largest banks.

My advancement and training I was later to learn was not going to be smooth. A co-worker, Mike, with whom I had become sufficiently friendly confided that the two vice-presidents who were supposed to be helping nurture my development had already, agreed on a pact not to help me up the very steep learning curve in the group. The ice was broken with Mike after working many late nights together and he confided that as a youngster at school in the New York area, he was bullied by a group of black students who took his lunch. I suspected that I was the first black person he had had the privilege to be close with. After hearing this tale many things fell in place for me about Mike and I respected him sharing this clearly traumatic early childhood experience having suffered something similar in the Isle of Wight. I did not share my own encounter with Mike but his candor did bring us closer as comrades in arms.

My goose nevertheless was cooked; I was pushing water up hill. It would be a near futile exercise to learn untutored the intricacies of analyzing bank balance sheets and the art of bank merger targets and acquisitions. I knew that building a career in investment banking would not work for me under these circumstances. This was a game I could not win and one in which I was heavily out-matched since I had no mentor on which to rely for guidance. The relevant vice-presidents had concluded that there was little value in wasting time with a young man who would pay little dividends in terms of the size of their dizzy bonuses, which they spent, an inordinate amount of time behind closed doors calculating. It was not long after this time that a number of the firm's professionals were implicated in various insider-trading scandals that rocked Wall Street. My boss Mary Sykes, however, did show great integrity, and stood by her commitment and that of the firm when I was hired to secure a Green Card for me.

After my analyst stint, Mary gave me Stephen Schwarzman's number to call for a possible position in his new venture with Pete Peterson, the firm's former head. I called Steve and he was very nice and explained that he and Pete were sharing a desk and phone and they had not yet decided what the name and needs of the firm would be. He said to call in a few months once they had an office and some basic infrastructure in place. I never did call.

A new market was developing at the time trading, i.e., buying and selling, the mountains of debt of developing countries like, Brazil, Mexico, Poland, and Nigeria. This was my opportunity, as then banker, Columbia Professor Peter Marber explained to me. Nigeria's debt based on fundamentals of its ability and willingness to pay should have been trading at a much higher price but due to "institutional racism", as he described it, the price was kept artificially low. It was an opportunity for astute investors to exploit this anomaly over the decade to come and to accumulate the debt on the premise that the market would finally recognize its real worth at three to four times its current price in the late-1980s.

OYIBOS

On April Fools' Day 1988, I resigned to start my own business, International Asset Transactions (IAT), from the living room of my Upper West Side apartment. My reserved and understated disposition and thoughtful approach did not translate well in the hungry viciously competitive environment of an investment banking firm. These were not virtues that were well understood nor from what I could discern desired at many investment banks at the time. Working for myself, I was free to set not only my own hours but my own agenda and goals. These were goals that would make positive changes to my life and also for Nigeria.

15. Manhattan

"No one should come to New York to live unless he [she] is willing to be lucky". – E.B. White

Living on the Upper West Side had some unintended consequences; I shopped at Fairway supermarket, a crowded jumbled shop with a wide variety of produce on offer and where shoppers jostled with their carts as if they were in a roller-derby. Caged in like rats in the shop's tight confines, shoppers were usually in a huge hurry to conclude their shopping and get out. While shopping for my weekly provisions, I was repeatedly harassed by shoppers young and old alike, male and female, asking for prices for items on the shelves or for me to bring them one thing or another from the shelf above assuming since I was a person of color that I must work there. "How much is this, is it on sale?" "I need six boxes of diapers over there on that shelf." This, even if I was wearing a suit and tie! Workers in the store wore white uniforms with name tags and caps with the store's name "Fairway" emblazoned in bright orange. This seemed of no consequence to those furiously grocery shopping. Initially I obliged until I realized there was a pattern here and the number of requests escalated beyond normal reason to the point that I might as well have worked there and at least be paid for my services. At one point it became so uncomfortable to shop at Fairway that I was driven to shop at D'Agostino Supermarkets, a rival larger chain next door that was not famed for the freshness and variety of its produce. I was marginalized and minimized in the store. Occasionally I encountered such problems elsewhere in New York although interestingly I cannot recall ever having such an encounter in any other city in the world outside America, including London where I grew up and faced other challenges. London was driven by minutely perceptible gradations of class and New York appeared driven by race and ethnicity. Shopping at Fairway Supermarket reinforced this and was an illuminating reminder that in America race frequently bubbles below the surface even on the Upper West Side of Manhattan the bastion of liberal thinkers in New York.

Save for this not so minor inconvenience, New York continued to grow on me and the quality of life in the city improved steadily, with working air-conditioning in all subway cars and the eradication of the graffiti that once blighted the city, along with the ubiquitous and aggressive pan-handlers I met on my arrival in 1985. New York is a city apart from America, a global citizen that measures itself with other great cities of the world like Hong Kong or Tokyo. Similarly, unlike heartland Americans, New Yorkers' indifference to their recent immigrant roots, whether from Sicily or Kansas tend to be New Yorkers first and Americans second. In this spirit I took driving lessons with a wry dry-humored Caribbean-American instructor to earn a coveted driving license for identification purposes. John was keen to dispel any illusions I might have about America from my closeted Ivy background. "I am going to take you to another America right here in New York," he said grinning. He took me for a drive through the most desolate and wretched sections of the Bronx where I witnessed playful children emerging from burnt-out urban hovels to fetch water from fire hydrants in plastic buckets. "Welcome to the other America". The scene resembled many I had seen in Nigeria, it provoked fear and came as a great unexpected tear rendering shock.

Manhattan

I was and remain close to my family and was in contact with them in London and Nigeria through visits, telephone calls, and regular old-fashioned letter correspondence. Family, however, were reluctant to visit New York, an unsafe city they viewed from the lenses of popular 1970s and '80s cop television dramas like Kojak and Hill Street Blues, which featured guns, violence, and desolate neighborhoods like those John had introduced me to. In those days' people in the U.K. and the British Commonwealth viewed America and Americans with a great deal of earnest suspicion and cynicism. This trepidation of vulgar cultural imperialism was later summed up in David Bowie's 1997 song, "I'm Afraid of Americans". Americans were not serious people; they were to be viewed as frivolous at best. Some concession however was given to achievements like NASA and the Apollo moon landing, as well as Clint Eastwood and Woody Allen movies. Moreover, against the order of things elsewhere in the world, Americans insisted on calling "football", soccer, and their rugby like game played with hands and an odd-shaped ball, football! Reductionism summoned up much of the world's view of America at the time and vice-versa.

I missed my family very much and pondered from time-to-time moving back to Europe to be near them but a visit to a favorite long forgotten restaurant, museum or other event, e.g., BAM, the Knicks (in their heyday) at Madison Square Garden, the Cloisters and MOMA, the sight of exhausted steaming foil-wrapped Marathon runners heading for the subway through autumn leaves on a cold blustery November day, or splendid summer concerts and fireworks in Central Park, would reinforce my desire to stay. New York still has a charm and certain glamour which if you can afford it makes it an unassailable village when compared to great colossal and truly cosmopolitan cities like London and even Paris or Rome to live in. It is a city where ordinary folk can regularly mingle and rub elbows with those of power, fame and fortune, as well as misfortune. New Yorkers think little of a brushing encounter at dinner with Woody Allen and his wife leaving as one arrives, finding Paul Newman, when he was alive, and his wife seated next to you at the Promenade Theatre on the Upper West Side taking in an off-Broadway show, or encountering a grinning Jack Nicholson with smart sunglasses seated on the same park bench, as if on the set of Batman, quietly watching his child playing on the climbing structures in a Central Park playground near Museum Mile as you watch yours.

    I nevertheless continued to struggle to find a quick response that would satisfy the curiosity of Americans who seemed to struggle with who I was. They were not accustomed to meeting a black individual, an American, from Africa with an English accent and educated at Harvard and the LSE. Some mistook my English reserve, without customary American presumptions of intimacy and familiarity, as a sign of evasive aloofness. I was not the open-book they were accustomed to. This perhaps unfairly, earned me an aura of mystery among some acquaintances. In America you have to show that you belong. In contrast to Europe where people understood who I was often just by seeing my face and hearing my voice, no other explanation was really necessary. There was a much broader and deeper tableau of Venn diagrams with logical relation between infinite collections of sets as compared to the finite selection I frequently encountered in America. I learned at work and leisure in America that it was important for people to be able to quickly put you in a box; this helped set their minds at ease whether you were friend or foe and worth bonding with. When they couldn't find the right box for me then trouble ensued as they struggled to squeeze me into boxes which by design were ill-fitting and caused further confusion and misunderstanding. I remember being invited out to the Hamptons one summer with a group of friends and as we headed back from the beach to shower and change for dinner the various guests chatted, "Networking". A young smart bookish looking Harvard Law School McKinsey consultant overheard me mention that my father had three wives and mouth agape, peppered me with questions how and what I felt about this. "Your father had three wives!" "Wow!" "Did they live in the same house?" "Was it weird having half-brothers and sisters or do you consider them like regular sisters and brothers?" He seemed unable to accept my straightforward explanation that it was not that uncommon among Nigerian's of a certain era and to that extent his rapid quick-fire questions had not merited a great deal of thought on my part, just like being black. It was not something I woke up and struggled with each morning like a new pair of tight fitting shoes. The experience however did teach me the importance of being able to explain deviations from the mean in American society in a succinct sound bite. Questions deemed highly personal and perhaps even rude and offensive in Europe are understood to be reflective of the cultural homogeneity of the nation and the healthy curiosity of its people.

16. Work and Adventure

Now free as my own boss I could work with whom I wanted and on projects that fitted my goals, values, and aspirations in life. As luck would have it my early cold calls were soon rewarded. I was elated to have been engaged by a major American consumer products company to arrange for the sale of several million U.S. dollars Nigerian debt. The company had accumulated the debt trading goods with local merchants. Armed only with my keen negotiating skills, telephone, and HP12C calculator, I earned a fee that was a multiple of my annual salary, bonus included at Shearson Lehman. My early exuberance however was short-lived; it would be almost six months before I was able to conclude another transaction, which was an instructive lesson in the unpredictability of an entrepreneur's income.

I soon became one of a handful of experts on Nigerian debt. For once who I was became a great asset for those outside. My advisory services were in much demand from multinational companies across the globe who were eager to have someone knowledgeable with integrity explain the debt accumulated on their books from goods sold to Nigeria during its oil boom years in the seventies. Oil and gas exports were Nigeria's primary means of obtaining hard currency to pay bills for its prodigious appetite for imported goods and services. As with many developing countries at the time, these bills for goods and services went unpaid as the country's oil revenues spectacularly collapsed from $25 billion in 1980, to $12 billion in 1982, and $6 billion in 1986. The situation became so dire for those waiting to be paid that I received a call from the irate treasurer of an American multinational. "Gus, this is not good enough, you need to get more phone lines." He was fuming because he was unable to reach me because my single telephone line was constantly busy. Back then it took the better part of a day of continuous dialing to successfully place a single brief and barely audible call to Nigeria. This rendered my single line busy for most of the working day. That afternoon I called the phone company to subscribe for the new call-waiting service; this however did not return me to the treasurer's good graces. The debt mandate was awarded elsewhere.

Fortunately for me, in between, I had concluded an extraordinary trade buying and selling Nigerian debt within minutes, from the London trading desk of Chemical Bank, and selling the same debt simultaneously at a gain back to their New York trading desk, which for reasons that were unclear to me, did not coordinate with their London colleagues. I was astonished that the two desks were quoting different prices for the same debt, which made it possible to buy from one and sell to the other and in the process realize a risk-less profit! It was a cheeky trade and I received a call from the bank's head of LDC trading with some choice expletives. Suffice it to say that the bank thereafter coordinated its trading on its New York and London desk. They should have paid me a king's ransom because in truth I gave the bank a cheap instructive lesson on the importance of coordinated global risk management.

1993, was a very busy and creative year for IAT. The firm completed one of the first ever financial securitizations in France. The transaction was so novel and unique that it required the consent of the French Ministry of Finance since France did not have any legislation governing the area. I commuted to Paris every few weeks for about 18 months and was advised by Air France that I was one of their most frequent transatlantic flyers. The airline rewarded me by assigning a dedicated person for my bookings and routinely upgraded me from business class to Concorde. The groundbreaking assignment was so stressful that the French law partner on the project unhappily suffered a heart attack and died the day after we closed. He had just returned to Paris, on Concorde, "So as not to waste time", to patriotically vote in the French elections. Ironically, he did not realize that his hurried supersonic dash was only to meet a premature death at the other end.

In the same year, the firm devised a program, which allowed billions of U.S. dollars of physically traded Nigerian debt (paper certificates) to trade electronically. This groundbreaking financial alchemy was a major game changer in the market. It allowed the debt for the first time to be eligible for trading and purchase by large institutional investors, e.g., Fidelity. Trading volume or liquidity in the debt increased more than tenfold, and the price rose sharply. Those fortunate enough to be holding the debt made significant fortunes. There were crude attempts to replicate the program by nimrod boffins at several investment banks, but such was its success that like the iPod, it became the ubiquitous market standard that even polymath market wizards could not undo. The product had the enormously advantageous and rare commodity among today's toxic financial derivatives of being uncomplicated. Like a cup or straw, its strength laid in its plain, practical, simplicity and utility.

The firm's innovation earned me the attention of the stately investment bank Morgan Stanley and my old school friend Mario Franciscotti. He invited me to interview for a position with the firm, which I did but was neither willing nor truly ready to give up my entrepreneurial and creative zeal for the rigid confines of an investment bank. This was the only time I considered seriously returning to work for an investment bank. Basically all the money in the world would probably not be sufficient for me to cross the Rubicon again. I did however extend a warm thanks to Mario for looking out for an old friend and schoolmate.

During this hectic period of innovation, I travelled frequently both for work and for leisure. In 1993, when I finally became an American citizen, I carefully pondered my new status. It meant in practical terms, being able to travel without endless tedious visas and no longer being referred to as an "Alien." I wondered if with my special commemorative green American passport, green unfortunately like my Nigerian passport, I would now be lumped into Americana or whether my identity would survive. My dual Nigerian and American citizenship notwithstanding, I have always felt more of a global citizen than the Nigerian, Nigerian-British, Nigeria-American, British or American monikers placed on me. First becoming part of one culture, mainstream English society, and then another almost as alien, America. Ultimately, I have chosen to forsake returning to a life of privilege in Nigeria for an independent career in America trying in my own inimitable way to build bridges to my country of birth, Nigeria, and that of my childhood and teenage years, England. In this spirit I have consciously chosen a professional and personal life that would take me to visit many countries and cultures. One such journey was to Argentina, where I was to learn that perhaps I was not as "worldly" as I thought.

I was picked up at the airport by two genial characters, one tall covered in prison like tattoos and the other short and very talkative. They did not speak English and I spoke only a few words of Spanish. I had been cautioned by my friends not to take an unmarked car and to only take a yellow cab to my hotel. Tired and feeling like a seasoned world traveler, I foolishly decided that these two characters were harmless and followed them into their unmarked car; after all they had already been good enough to take my heavy luggage from me even without my asking. As they drove they pointed out sites of interest, the mayor's residence, the town hall and so on until we were near the deserted docks. They asked if I had changed currency at the airport and I said yes and showed them a wad of local currency, the equivalent of several hundred U.S. dollars. They asked to check and make sure that I had been given the new and not the old currency and I consented having been distracted by the driver's large tattooed partner. The driver returned what seemed like the same wad and then gunned the car into the docks, screeching to a sudden halt as if in a movie car chase. He then said what sounded to me like "I have a wife". I congratulated him on this remarkable achievement but he became even more agitated. "Do you have any children?" I asked politely. Whereupon it became evident to me that things were being lost in translation. The large tattooed fellow jumped out and rather unceremoniously dropped my bags on the pavement. I thanked them and offered a twenty-dollar tip for their kindness, which they duly accepted before racing off up the road tires spinning leaving rubber and smoke behind. I glanced around and noticed the area seemed desolate and isolated. I struggled with my bag until I found a policeman who directed me to the Hotel Claridge some miles away. I thought it must be a new hotel and that perhaps that's why my drivers dropped me at the wrong location, it was not until I repeatedly counted my local currency that I realized the wad I now had was the equivalent of about one U.S. dollar. I finally realized that the muggers were agitated because they were telling me they had a "knife" which did not engender the reaction of fear they were no doubt expecting. Deeming me crazier than they, they sped off with my money leaving me stranded and unaware of my mugging and brush with possible death or injury. At the precise moment of my epiphany the news on the television was reporting on gangs that were fleecing gullible gringo tourists arriving at the airport. So much for the battle stripes I thought I had gained from being a veteran of Murtala Muhammad International Airport.

I was reminded yet again of the difficulties of passing seamlessly into different worlds on a trip to Caracas. I had lost touch with my friend Antonio Maldonado-Camera after we had moved on to college and was surprised to receive a call from him in New York. He was working in marketing for Warner-Lambert in Venezuela where he returned after studying in London and tracked me down in the phone book having been told by our mutual friend Charlie Etame that I was now resident in New York. We were both very happy to reconnect after so many years and he invited me to Caracas for that summer. When the time came I ventured to the Venezuelan Consulate midtown to obtain my visa since I was still holding a Nigeria Passport, I did not become a U.S. citizen until 1993. On arrival in Caracas, the passport control officials were incredulous that a Nigerian would be visiting their country on vacation; they accorded me the warmest welcome I think I have ever received at any border and sent one of their colleagues to escort and expedite my passage through customs formalities since for all intense and purposes I spoke no Spanish. It was only later that Antonio pointed out that they probably thought I was a high-ranking delegate from OPEC as the international oil cartel meetings were being held in Caracas that week.

Antonio was there to meet me, smiling, looking youthful and genial as always. As we drove with his pretty and energetic girlfriend Carolina he explained that we had to detour by subway to run a quick errand. Because of the city's unbelievable traffic fueled like Lagos by petrodollars it was quicker to go by subway. We parked in a car park near the subway and continued to the platform as Carolina explained that you have to be quick because the doors on the subway close very rapidly. In a flash I was marooned on the platform as the train sped out of the station, left with no local currency, no idea where I was and without Antonio's address or phone number all of which were in my luggage in the car. A strange feeling of shrinking isolation came over me as all that I knew about Venezuela vanished with the train. I immediately jumped on the next train with the hope of finding them at the subsequent stop. Meanwhile Antonio and Carolina had disembarked and were headed back to where I had been. We continued this dance back-and-forth for about an hour or more before I found a station where they spoke some English and kindly agreed to make an announcement on the system that Antonio should come and pick me up. To my relief, he did. There was much laughter as we drove to Antonio's mother Dora's apartment. That night to celebrate we dined at El Portico a fabulous Italian restaurant and took in a performance of American jazz musician George Benson at the Tamanaco hotel. The aged and charming Dora gave me a tourist guide around Caracas while Antonio was at work and sweetly held my hand, as if I were a schoolboy, as we crossed the road outside the local Parliament buildings. Antonio later told me that my patient listening to his mother's many amusing tales of her diplomatic travels with her deceased squash-buckling ambassador husband told to me in Spanish and Italian with a tiny bit of English earned me a reward. Dora, deeming me saintly had apparently strategically placed a rosary under my mattress in the guest bedroom in protection of my virtuous soul. This is probably as close as I will get to being canonized, but my behavior was consistent with the reverence I learnt in Nigeria and at Finchley to accord the upmost respect to the elderly.

I returned to Caracas each summer thereafter usually with my latest prospective girlfriend, each very different from the other. I was struck by the stark parallels between Venezuela's economic and political fortunes and those of Nigeria. Both countries were major oil exporters, although Nigeria's population was significantly larger and the poverty more stark. Venezuela also brought back memories of my days as a youth in Nigeria. The country had the same carefree innocence of Nigeria in the early sixties and pockets of unparalleled natural beauty. Islands like the stunning secluded Sombrero and Boca Seca where I sailed with Antonio and his charming beautiful wife Angelica and their infant son, Alex. En route to Morrocoy where the yacht was anchored we passed through the idyllic palm tree lined coast line of Tucacas barely touched by modernity with its delightful little villages with ramshackle houses painted in bright tropical colors. We snorkeled and swam among shoals of spectacular iridescent tropical fish, (I might add with my floatation devise firmly strapped on), in the pristine crystal blue waters of the Caribbean. These stunning spots had not been found by tourists and in any event could only be reached by boat.

OYIBOS

Back in Caracas we dressed, ready to explore one of the city's excellent dining establishments. Antonio lived in a building where the country's joint-chief of staff for the armed forces lived. The building as a result had an honorary guard in the form of a young lamb-faced military trainee with whom we exchanged daily banter. He was stationed at the front-gate with his machine gun slung casually across his shoulder. With each successive visit, rather like Nigeria, the economy was deteriorating and there were more-and-more reports of lawlessness in Caracas. Before we descended downstairs in the elevator we heard what sounded like a rapid burst of gunfire, when we opened the front door to the building, the ashen faced guard slumped into the foyer with several fresh, steaming and blackened bullet holes visible through his military uniform. The floors were covered with a scarlet pool. He had managed to make it to the door from the gate some thirty feet away. Angelica, a surgeon in training, tended the wounded soldier as best she could but life had already left his young body. In shock we retreated to their apartment to ponder what to do after calling the emergency services and police who were soon at the scene. These events were becoming so frequent that the residents shrugged and quickly moved on with their lives. We finally went for a very sober last supper, which preceded an early morning flight back to New York. The incident contrasted vividly with the jollity of the preceding days. This violent encounter like that of my childhood left me shaken, it brought back memories I had long forgotten about the fragility and sometimes seemly low worth of life in Nigeria. At the same time it made me even more resigned to the fact that death can be untimely even for the most innocent. I was appreciative that life is a fleeting gift best enjoyed

Work and Adventure

before the end. Not long after that Antonio was given a transfer posting by his new employers to New York. This was the last of many memorable sailing visits to Caracas.

My love affair with South America continued in spite of my sobering Venezuelan encounter. While its violence confirmed to me how close I could be to death, another visit demonstrated how one's looks can radically alter the reception you encounter, one day under one set of circumstances mistaken for a shop clerk at Fairway and under another as an esteemed prosperous OPEC delegate. The magic mirror of identity was again at work. I journeyed to Brazil on business where exhausted after a day of battling Sao Paulo traffic, my colleague and I decided to head to town for a slap-up dinner at the city's finest Italian restaurant. We enquired of the very attractive Japanese-Brazilian concierge if the restaurant accepted credit cards; she confirmed yes and arranged for a cab to take us to the establishment. The food and wine were exquisite. My colleague and fellow diner was similarly of African descent, hailing from Gambia. Judging from the initial countenance of the maître d' one would guess that they did not receive guests from the African Continent very often. In any event, it seems they had concluded that we were diplomats and decided to pull-out all the stops and to spare no expense in entertaining us. When the bill arrived, having only a limited amount of local currency on our persons I casually proffered my American Express card only to be met by blank disappointed from the waiter. He motioned to his superior. By this time we were the last guests left in the restaurant and the waiters ran to block the exits to secure the means of egress. My colleague and I prepared for a long evening washing dishes. Finally, the manager called the concierge at the hotel who sent a messenger with cash to pay for our delicious meal, at which point we were released from captivity into the humid Sao Paolo night and whisked back to our hotel by our taxi driver into the arms of the waiting and apologetic concierge.

National borders and crossings for me are a metaphor for who we are and how others see us. The color of your passport notwithstanding, the habitually terse reception of border officials can either affirm or disabuse you of any conception you may have about your nationality, identity, and its worth. I visited my college roommate Bharat every year in Geneva, Switzerland where he was working for WIPO after Duke Law School and later for the luxury goods group, Richemont owners of Cartier. On one visit after presenting my Nigerian passport the customs official looked at my tanned leather briefcase bulging with work documents from various meeting in London and Paris and asked if I had anything to declare. I said, "No". He again asked "anything to declare" in French this time and again I replied "No". Unconvinced and trying to look discrete he directed his eyes squarely at my briefcase. I said, "No" again and we danced like this for about twenty minutes before he finally decided to allow me to pass into arrivals with a nod and a wink as if to say: "Just doing my job to ensure the appropriate red carpet welcome for fleeing dictators with bags of loot to enrich the coffers of Swiss banks". I was livid as I was in Fairway that I was once again being unfairly pigeonholed. At least these border officials were kinder than the many others I met on my travels.

UK border control used to hold me up precisely because of my polished (Mrs. Black) English accent, which contradicted in their minds how an American should sound. They took the preposterous comical position, rather ironically I thought, that I was actually masquerading as an American and was really secretly resident in the U.K. illegally. I took great glee in disabusing them of their assumed intrigue and brandished my American passport with extra pride leaving them even more befuddled!

The French were, as one might expect, much more amusing. Looking at my West African face, they tore at my American passport to see if it was a fake and then handed it back in near shreds officiously telling me "Monsieur", "La prochaine fois, vous ne serez pas autorisé à entrer dans le pays avec ce passeport mutilé." ("Sir", "You will not be allowed into the country next time with this mutilated passport"). I was out of the presumed box, and was obliged to apply for a new passport having had my old passport torn literally apart. As if this was not enough reproof, for good measure, I was sent with a knowing superior Gallic smile, for a brief interrogation in a windowless anteroom. There various colleagues were summoned to pass judgment, by way of a doctor's second opinion, on my mutilated passport and to give an air of seriousness to the unfolding irksome Comédie-Française.

The biggest border offenders were until a few years ago the surly U.S. Customs and Immigrations officials who delighted in tearing apart the luggage of anybody born in Nigeria with reckless abandon in search of non-existent contraband. I was convinced that like Wall Street traders their salaries were bonus-based. They earned more the more drug smugglers they apprehended. When I became a U.S. citizen, I thought the red carpet would be my new airport greeting, but on seeing my mutilated passport we were back to the routine. Somebody high up must have realized the inappropriateness of this un-American and barbaric behavior because the practice finally abruptly stopped ironically at the turn of the New Millennium. The phrase welcome home took on a new meaning for me, it was nice not to fear or worry about gun-wearing bigoted Stasi like law enforcement officials who as a taxpayer were actually supposed to be working for me and countless other Americans.

The Christmas 2009 failed exploits of the Nigerian "underpants bomber" I hope will not reopen this long closed chapter of indiscriminate searches for those of Nigerian provenance, particularly for me since I was born in the same town of Kaduna, though decades apart, in another era when underwear meant intimate apparel worn to protect nether regions and not as a weapon for wanton slaughter. "The Sea has drowned the fish", as Nigerians, say when baffled by contradictory circumstances.

There was nothing though like 9/11 to call into question attitudes about identity, being American and being other. I was walking on Paris's Champs-Élysées with friend and colleague Adam Dixon when he received a call from his mother in Connecticut. She said a plane had crashed into the World Trade Center and that we should find a television as soon as possible to follow events. We rushed to our hotel in the 8th Arrondissement on Rue d'Astorg to find many guests sullen and an eerie air about us. We went upstairs and watched the unfolding tragedy on CNN in shock and disbelief while desperately trying to reach loved ones on our cell phones to no avail. I was stuck in Europe for almost two weeks, which gave me ample opportunity to absorb and observe the outpouring of world sympathy. Thankfully all were safe back in New York, although understandably shocked. In a gesture of kindness the likes I probably will never experience again in France, the manager of the hotel wrote a handwritten note of sympathy and support to every American guest, including me, at the hotel. We were extended the keys to the heart of the French people; there was a heartfelt outpouring of grief for America's loss. Unfortunately this was soon put into reverse with the well-documented megalomaniac policy missteps of the George W. Bush administration. His administration tragically squandered a unique moment in history for America to triumph without firing a single shot in anger. The West African term: "Small boys with strong minds", comes to attention when I think of this missed opportunity to corral the vast majority of the world behind America. They served much-derided Bonga, a scrawny bony fish, to the world. It was a misguided response of Herculean proportions to a modern tragedy. Adam later reminded me that prophetically I had turned down an attractively priced lease for an office space on the hundred-and-tenth floor of one of the Twin Towers some years before after the first terrorist attack in 1993, fearing precisely that, another deadly strike.

Meanwhile back in New York the individual tasked with manning my office, Mohammed, a French-Moroccan with a dusky North African complexion had fled into semi-hiding in fear for his life. I managed to track him down after several days of frantic calls to his home and cell phone. He was shaken and genuinely feared for his life. I had empathy and sympathy for his dilemma, rendered hostile in his chosen home not by his words or deeds but simply because of his background and ethnicity.

There were many strange incidents and challenges that I encountered over my twenty-one years since I founded the firm but perhaps the strangest and most disturbing concerned an interview candidate that we liked and were going to call back to make a possible offer. I later heard about him on the evening news. Not having found a job for months and deeply depressed the candidate stepped in front of an oncoming train in New Jersey not knowing we were going to call him back for a final interview. IAT was one of several firms where he had sought or was seeking work. The incident was very upsetting for all concerned at the firm but there was little we could have done, since he showed no signs of depression at his interviews.

Throughout my professional working career, the French border control notwithstanding, I have always been accorded the highest professional respect in France, and have found the French willing to take risks on my talent when British or American institutions were unwilling. Like my early experience in the City of London, Americans by-and-large, have shown until more recently great reluctance to take a punt on persons of color in meaningful professional roles on Wall Street, as evidenced by my putative mentors at Shearson Lehman back in the day. I always felt rightly or wrongly that many had concluded statistically that the risk-rewards were simply not merited for them to act otherwise. Not the bigotry of Fairway that surfaces under strain like laboratory rats but more of a greed calculus devoid of all colors but green with dollar signs. Professor Peter Marber's "institutional racism" comments continue to ring to mind, although my hopes and those of others, even on Wall Street, abide with the election of President Obama, Nobel Laureate. Societal change however as I have witnessed in Nigeria more-often-than-not requires generations over many, many, decades. In England because the legacy of the empire mentality lived on until the empire came to

Work and Adventure

Britain's doorstep in the New Millennium as what I would term reverse colonialization, initiated by my father and his generation, local blue-eyed boys were undoubtedly until relatively recently the preferred way to go. The French for reasons I have not been fully able to comprehend appear more readily to look, at least for those trained outside France or its colonies, at the merits and rigor of the intellectual thought of that individual, as well as their sensitivity to the uniquely French approach to life and business. As a result, France has played a large role in my professional fortunes for which I am eternally grateful. This is something that I have frequently discussed with my cartoon writer friend in Paris, Jeffrey Kearney over a glass of Bordeaux; a Frenchman through marriage but a Kentuckian-New Yorker at heart. All of this I might add despite my having only a rudimentary ability to speak the language, Mrs. Black would have been astonished.

17. Uncompromising Friendship

"While Westerners tend to shed family members, Africans greedily gather and hoard them" (*The Times*, of London, December 29, 2009).

For me family extends much further than the nuclear family, embracing aunts, uncles, first, second, and third cousins, close family friends, and beyond. Family in the West African tradition brings with it burdens and demands that are rarely seen or understood in the Western context. These demands often manifest themselves in the form of monetary help for education and other material needs including traditional celebrations like weddings and burials. Such demands cannot be refused without fear of admonition from the family clan. Similarly in England the concept of a "mate" (friend) I have found to be much deeper in my experience than that of a "buddy" in the American context. A "mate" is a friend for whom you would take a bullet. A "buddy" is someone you go to ballgames with and have beers with afterwards. My friendship with Bharat is reflective of the former, that unique amalgam of my New Commonwealth and British values. This theme or trait can lead to uncompromising levels of trust that would confound most Americans and which often results in interesting repercussions as you will see below.

I have been fortunate to have many mates (close friends) in my life but none have been as mystical and comical as my friendship with my Indian guru friend Bharat. The first time I visited Bharat in Geneva; he was embarking on a ski expedition with friends to Chamonix and insisted that I join them. I protested that I had no skies and only my light gabardine raincoat. Bharat said: "That's fine, you'll be okay", and

Uncompromising Friendship

with the trusting acceptance of a close mate or family, we headed for the mountains, passport in hand to cross the French border. Needless to say I nearly froze to death and tumbled down the mountain on borrowed skis while the locals looked on at this crazy foreign fellow rolling down the mountain and almost breaking his neck crashing into a tree. I was sure I had fractured my thumb but in stoic fashion I soldiered on now on foot down the mountain.

The scene was repeated again years later, this time in Crans-Montana, Switzerland, where while cross-country skiing, I neglected to ask Bharat how to navigate a sharp bend and promptly fell and dislocated my shoulder. I stupidly did not seek treatment until I was back in New York. The specialist asked which helicopter company medivacked me off the mountain and I explained as I was taught in my Finchley days that I simply popped my shoulder back myself and quietly suffered the unbearable pain thereafter until I visited his surgery, admittedly with a few stiff drinks and painkillers in-between. Astonished he explained that if I had delayed treatment much longer I would have permanently lost the motion in my left shoulder. I was stuck in daily physical therapy for six months. I recounted these tales to friends who were aghast at my dangerous folly, skiing downhill for the first time in Chamonix's dangerous glacier feared by accomplished skiers never mind new starters like me.

The following summer Bharat dragged me up Mont Blanc in the same raincoat, admiring the Swiss Alps and ignoring my protests that we should head-down the mountain before dark. Accepting, I followed blindly and sure enough darkness soon descended. Frozen, we crawled down the mountain literally on our hands and knees for fear of falling off the path into the abyss below. Bharat laughed with a mischievous grin once we had reached the bottom of the mountain alive and in one piece with faculties' more-or-less intact. We drove to a spa, with hot springs to relax my frayed nerves and frozen body. At moments on the mountain I thought it would be touch-and-go with Swiss rescue teams with Saint Bernard dogs with brandy barrels around their necks looking for our frozen carcasses on Mont Blanc.

After these incidents above, I was very, very careful to examine and consider Bharat's invitations before saying yes. His wedding in Delhi, India was one I could not say no to and provided the usual fun and drama. Bharat had arranged lodging for my family and other guests at the very economical Maharaja Guest House. It was there that I made the rookie mistake on arrival of tipping a month's salary of about $5. The hotel staff thereafter camped outside our door and took it upon themselves to burst repeatedly into our room throughout the night to ask if we required any services in the hope of another month's salary. My misstep was a poignant reminder of what a difference a few dollars of thoughtful generosity makes for most of the world outside of Europe and America.

The wedding was a splendid affair held over several days, the highlight of which was the bride and groom arriving on top of elephants adorned with bright colored paint. After riding atop elephants, as one does when in India, we departed for Goa to recover from Delhi Belly, acute diarrhea. Goa reminded me of the Caribbean other than for the abundant cows (of the bovine variety) wondering up-and-down freely on the beautiful beaches admiring Western hippy tourists who failed to find their way home from their primitive excursion into the psychedelia decades earlier.

Several nights at the magnificent, and now infamous, Taj in Mumbai prepared us for our return home but only after taking a trip back in time at the Gymkhana Club. The Gymkhana Club was a vestige of the colonial era and the days of the Raj. I took tea on the club's verandah and drifted back in time while taking-in some excellent cricket on the club's immaculate lawns. This was all thanks to the kind hospitality of some friends of a college friend who I met in Lagos some years prior. At the airport the customs official noting in my passport that I was born in Nigeria, instantly did his best impression of a customs official at Murtala Muhammad International Airport hands extended for a bribe, which was met by a cool icy gaze from me.

Bharat's coup de grâce was a breakfast meeting at Geneva's swank Hotel President Wilson. He had organized a meeting for me with a friend-of-a-friend who was reputed to be the smartest private banker on the planet. We had breakfast in the hotel's plush foyer, which was filled with the sound of clanging utensils and the babble of exotic languages. The gentleman in question was a tall young bearded Bostonian, who looked more like a tree-hugger than a brilliant affluent Swiss banker. Sporting the ubiquitous Bling-bling timepiece that is synonymous with his profession, he stroked his beard with the air of confidence of a man with a charmed existence. He then embarked on a rambling monologue about why, in his opinion, Swiss bankers were clueless about the business of private banking. He claimed that he had Merlin's magical wand and could unlock the Eldorado promised by as yet undiscovered modern Swiss private banking practices, but gave no hints what that was.

Ignoring his immense ego, I tried as best as I could to contain my boredom. This while at the same time disregarding the impatient circadian rhythms from my jet-lagged body to fall asleep right-there-

and-then curled-up in the very comfortable deep beige leather lounge chair I was sitting in. After enduring almost an hour of drivel, and cold expensive and overdone scrambled eggs, we parted company with a limpid handshake and a Shakespearean hail-fellow well met exchange. Brad had the distracted air of an affable but troubled young man. He seemed far from the brilliant wonder kid I had been told to expect. We waived goodbye and he leisurely vanished outside. I wondered what the encounter was all about. I watched as he walked past revving super-cars to his Porsche. He sped-off down Lac Léman's winding lakefront road. I left by my accustomed foot transport and walked briskly by the lake nestled against the backdrop of beautiful snowcapped mountains, and the wind-blown spray of the shooting jet d'eau (jet-plume of water). I was none the wiser about Swiss institutional money managers, which was my own stated mission.

 The next time I saw Brad; his mug shot was emblazoned on the front page of The New York Times. Apprehended apparently by the U.S. federal authorities for aiding citizens evade millions in taxes through Swiss bank accounts. Among his reported exploits was smuggling precious diamonds for his clients in toothpaste tubes. He turned state's evidence pulling down with him a good chunk of Switzerland's infamous bank secrecy clientele. Brad no doubt also surrendered other secret tricks of his trade. The newspapers said that he was seeking a multi-million U.S. dollar whistleblower reward for his collaboration with the authorities. Extraordinary chutzpah by any accounts! I guess this could have been considered a revolution in Swiss private banking but it was certainly not what I had imagined. I pondered if he was "wired" by his handlers like in the movies during my brief uneventful encounter with infamy. Come to think of it, he did have a disappointed look as he left. I was not the stereotyped son of a Nigerian army general with ill-gotten billions that he was perhaps expecting to boost his portfolio of dodgy felonious American clients. Bharat once again had succeeded in maintaining his perfect record of securing my uncompromising trust, and unwittingly revealing his own vulnerability to the same incurable quirk.

18. Building Bridges

In spite of my desire to remain un-tethered to one particular culture or identity, I find myself always called back to my first home, Nigeria.

I made many journeys to Nigeria over the years after I had started IAT and had many memorable incidents. The pioneer country fund I had started back in 1993, Nigeria Emerging Market Fund, was the first ever dedicated offshore fund for Nigeria. Country funds were relatively fashionable in the 1990s and there were funds for new emerging economies like Brazil, Mexico, and China. Although specialized initially in Nigerian debt it went on in the late-nineties to become the largest investor in the Nigerian Stock Exchange (NSE). The fund was a founding investor in the country's Central Securities Clearing System Limited (CSCS), which was a critical component in the evolution and modernization of Nigeria's stock market. I was a member of the board of the CSCS, although for practical reasons, I did not attend any meetings and eventually stepped-down. I was, however, glad that through our groundbreaking investment, IAT was able to participate in the expansion and growth of the country financial markets. Somewhat like our earlier success making the country's debt tradable for big global investors, the CSCS made it easier for foreign institutional investors to buy and sell local stocks and bonds, attracting much needed foreign investment. Making obscure financial obligation tradable has been in part my professional mission for three decades. The success of the CSCS, coupled with the global economic boom, propelled a surge in trading volumes in Nigerian stocks over the next decade.

I had to travel frequently to Nigeria to meet with the Central Bank, Ministry of Finance, the NSE, local banks and leading companies. These trips were always marked by a new unexpected adventure. My father clearly enjoyed my visits and learned over the years to be very proud of his Harvard and LSE graduate son who worked in finance in New York. However he lamented that I no longer stayed with him on Mainland Lagos and preferred instead to stay at the Eko Meridian hotel in Victoria Island near my friends and in closer proximity to my meetings. It also left me unfettered from his third wife Florence with whom he lived and had the added advantage of keeping me from having to negotiate hours of traffic and choking pollution. I found it hard to connect with Florence, a widow with no children, who clearly wanted intimacy in the home she was building with her newly acquired husband.

On one visit I discovered that my Nigerian passport had expired and had to be renewed for me to return to New York. The passport office apparently had unbelievably run-out of passport booklets. I found myself in Lagos for almost one-month instead of the planned one week before my father revealed that he knew the head of the passport office and within a day I had my new passport. My father, despite his ill business fortunes at the time, was very well connected and liked, but had always shied away from using his connections unduly for his children preferring for us to make our own way in the world. Father was not a believer in the culture of illicit favors quaintly termed locally as: "as-man-know-man". I suspected that his touching hope was that I would decide to stay in Lagos indefinitely, which was not to be. I had already resolved to make my life in America.

I received a fax somewhat out of the blue one day from the then Finance Minster to come for a meeting in Abuja, the new capital and seat of government; presumably I thought to discuss Nigeria's debt on which I had become somewhat of an expert. I arrived at the minister's office, which had the usual sleepy air of most government ministries and was ushered into a waiting room where I sat with various other assorted local and foreign guests for five hours without an audience. I was finally told that the Minister having summoned me from New York was no longer able to meet as scheduled. Fuming and despondent, I continued to the airport where I met my college friend Emeka Dike who was in conversation with some business acquaintances. It turned out to be the head of the Board for Mobil Nigeria who attended the same church as Emeka and his Treasurer. Emeka introduced me and explained that I worked in finance in New York and had been an analyst at Shearson Lehman. The head of the Board then invited Emeka and me to fly back to Lagos with them on the Mobil corporate plane. I accepted their offer, which was better than waiting around for a flight that may not arrive and for which my seat may have been sold several times over. Commercial flights in Nigeria then were an ordeal, which started for those lucky enough to actually hold a boarding pass, with a chaotic scrambling foot-race with fellow passengers young and old to the aircraft in the hope of securing any seat possible; usually not their assigned seat. Civil servants, soldiers, executives, school children, members of the clergy, and market women with their merchandise all jostled playing musical chairs until it was evident that there were no seats for those left standing. They in turn had to disembark to resume their wait for the next flight, whenever that might be.

Once on board, the Mobil executives explained that the company needed to raise several hundred million U.S. dollars of funding for Oso II, a condensate project that Mobil Nigeria was looking to develop.

Building Bridges

While they had the support of head office in Fairfax, Virginia for the project, funds were not available in the company budget nor did it look like monies would be forthcoming from Nigeria its Joint-Venture (JV) partner. I said that I would think of a solution and get back to them, which I did some weeks later. Through my research, I found out that Mobil in Australasia had faced a similar dilemma solved by the local entity issuing its own notes or bonds independent of head office. I outlined the plan and travelled to Nigeria several times to present how the financing could be accomplished. I was confident the debt could be placed since I knew many of the financial institutions who already owned high yielding Nigerian government debt and were keen to have other similar quality exposure. I even travelled to Virginia to coach the Treasurer ahead of his presentation to senior management at Headquarters. His presentation was a success, the plan was approved but I was told that head office had baulked at IAT being the advisor and instead our unpaid ground breaking work notwithstanding the mandate would go to Credit Suisse First Boston (CSFB), who had a Nigerian managing director, a bright and very experienced project finance banker. To add insult to injury, I received an urgent call from Mobil on the day of the placement to say that CSFB had not been able to place sufficient notes/bonds and could I help with additional investors. A call from a CSFB MBA acolyte Associate followed shortly thereafter reconfirming what I already knew from Mobil. The upshot from what I understood was with a gun to their heads from Mobil, CSFB had to buy at least half the issuance. Justice of sorts but a valuable lesson on the importance of protecting ones intellectual property, like my mother I was often too generous of heart in my business dealings with various

Velociraptors. IAT's unrewarded pro-bono contribution was a significant aid in ensuring the growth of Nigeria's condensate exports.

I was invited to speak at a conference in Lagos on emerging market economic reform sometime in the late nineties, the conference was sponsored by a group of local banks eager for Nigeria to return to open economic reforms abandoned by the president Ibrahim Babangida or IBB as he was more popularly known, after a failed coup attempt on his life made him more guarded about both himself and what went on within Nigeria's borders. Rumor was that Babangida had agreed for the conference to go ahead only at the last moment after much lobbying from various advisors. My speech on Nigerian debt and opportunities for economic change seemed to have hit a cord with certain segments of the audience and numerous attendees seeking a private audience rushed me afterwards. The recurring theme or sub-text was my level of enthusiasm to run under their political banner, politics and parties technically having been banned. This was the one time I was actually afraid in Nigeria. I was afraid because they were seeking a commitment from me to Nigeria that I was unable to give and that might entail my life if I was not mindful of the military plain-clothes security agents in the audience. My intentions were to explain how economic change had been accomplished elsewhere in countries like Brazil not to stir up political fervor. I had failed to recognize the power of my dual or tri-identity and that there were people present in the audience who simply saw as I spoke on the podium, a Nigerian face in whom they trusted with a vision in line with their own aspirations for a better future for Nigeria and who they perhaps could trust to play a lead.

Building Bridges

My speech had aroused a pent-up passion for change that they had not had an opportunity to voice. I suspected that this was the very impulse that made Babangida hesitant in the first place to sanction the conference; he knew precisely that this might be the case. I would have liked to have met Babangida to find out what really was going through his mind and if my hunch was correct. He was for me one of Nigeria's most intriguing leaders and is still a power broker in the country today. I maintained a low profile thereafter at the conference although some still sought me out and called or came to my hotel room. It remains a dilemma that I periodically wrestle with how to stay connected with Nigeria but not be directly politically involved since many peers and contemporaries are now in high places in industry and politics.

My open and candid views on the country earned me a sound reputation among the country's technocrats and an invitation to a conference sponsored by the Central Bank of Nigeria's Debt Management Office. In that singularly Nigerian way, after completing my presentation and answering questions, I was ushered aside by an official from the CBN who told me that I would be an unscheduled guest of the government for two days in Abuja to deliver my presentation to the most senior officials of the CBN together with Joyce Chang Salomon Brother's star emerging market analyst who is now at JP Morgan. It was an invitation that could not be refused, other engagements elsewhere notwithstanding. Despite being based in America, like my father the country's officials recognized my roots in Nigeria and saw it as my national duty to provide these services, all gratis I might add, save for two traditional northern leather poufs that the CBN governor presented me for my efforts that I have in my living room today. The door in some ways was and I suspect is still open for me to play a part in Nigeria's future.

As a child, Nigeria's first president, Zik, visited our house on several occasions, he was a town's man and liked me because we shared the same birthday and were both born in northern Nigeria. As an adult I met two Nigerian Heads of State, the genial and agreeable Earnest Shonekan, lawyer and industrialist who succeeded Ibrahim Babangida after the fiasco M.K.O. Abiola elections which precipitated the arrival of strong-arm Dictator General Sani Abacha. I asked a banker in Lagos why Shonekan failed to hold power and he replied that Shonekan was "power shy" in a country where the Oga is only respected if he or she shows ruthless strength; something his defense secretary General Sani Abacha knew only too well. I had similar hints of such from the late Colonel Joe Garba who announced the coup d'etat that ousted head of state, General Yakubu Gowon in July 1975. Garba was Gowon's head of security! Joe was a graduate student when I was an undergraduate at Harvard and occasionally invited Nigerian students to his apartment or office to listen to reflections on his military and diplomatic life in Nigeria. Visiting his cramped office was like a game of chess, he had his guest chair in front of his desk placed at an awkward angle to test, he revealed later to me, how each visitor would address the situation; whether they sat uncomfortably wedged against the wall or asked him to adjust his desk so they could sit comfortable. This was one of many tests he used to gauge the mettle of would be adversaries, learnt no doubt from his military school training at Mons and Camberley in England. I found Joe both unnerving and a bit spooky and I suspected that perhaps he might have bullied those who were unfortunate not to have a strong will like mine. He was from all accounts a seasoned insider in the art of coup making in Nigeria; perhaps understandably given the above, he served as Federal Commissioner for External Affairs under Olusegun Obasanjo. When I saw him last in 1988 when he was Nigeria's representative at the United Nations (UN), he was kind enough to present to me an autographed copy of his book Diplomatic Soldiering. An active anti-apartheid campaigner while at the UN, he died in 2002 in Nigeria.

Obasanjo uniquely served both as a military (February 1976 to October 1, 1979), and subsequently as a civilian head of state. I attended an intimate New York lunch with him organized by a group of young professional Nigerians during which he could barely contain his eagerness to return to Nigerian politics after a long hiatus away from power, on returning to Nigeria he was allegedly implicated in a coup plot against the then head of state Sani Abacha who promptly imprisoned Obasanjo. Abacha's death saw Obasanjo released from jail where he emerged a born again Christian after probably enduring untold hardship and punishment while in jail. He subsequently returned to the presidency for two terms from May 1999 to May 2007 as a civilian head of state.

In 1998, I was invited to the memorial service for a college and LSE friend's prominent lawyer father and on entering his mother's Eastside apartment; I noted men with walkie-talkies and radio earphones with tell-tale curly white cords. These men would turn out to be Secret Service Agents. His mother introduced someone she described simply as "my friend Hillary" who was the First Lady, Hillary Rodham Clinton. She asked about my background obviously having seen West Africa in my face. We talked at some length about

Nigeria; she seemed both eager and able to listen and asked questions of my thoughts on US-Nigerian relations. I was candid, as I had learnt from Elliot Cohen and suggested that relations might be warmer beyond oil exports if there was more genuine, open, and constructive dialogue between the two countries. I was delighted when she accepted the position of Secretary of State under the Obama Administration and am cautiously optimistic that our chat will bode well for a deeper and more substantive relationship between Nigeria and my adoptive country.

I have long concluded that in Nigeria visions for corruption free plural democracy, a vibrant and robust free market based economy with modern infrastructure would take generations to fulfill. Like America at the turn of the century, there is still a Wild West frontier mentality in Nigeria, which plays out in all elements of daily life where gatekeepers abound at every corner extracting a toll from all who pass. The idea of statesmanship and civic order has still to be inculcated in the country's leadership at every level; it would be naïve to think otherwise and any commitment on my part as a future catalyst for economic change would henceforth be with this realization in mind. This was something I believe my father had grasped relatively early in his own professional career.

The next time I was to be in Nigeria was in February 2005 for my father's burial.

19. The Burial

It was at Regi's wedding that I saw how much tradition mattered to my father and the immense joy he had planning, entertaining, and feeding several hundred of our closest relatives and numerous throngs of other distant relatives and Onitsha kinsfolk. We were in Onitsha to celebrate and for the first time he could proudly share and showoff all but one of his children, Sam, to Onitsha. Sammy could not attend unfortunately because he had just lost his father-in-law in London. He reveled in the nuances of Onitsha wedding traditions, the payment of the symbolic dowry, kola nuts, and palm wine. Procuring victuals, sheep, cattle and goats for the festivities, as well as arranging transport and housing for all family guests while in Onitsha. He and Regi prepared our family compound and enlisted cousins, uncles and aunts, in-laws to cook and organize masquerades and singing troupes to entertain merry dancing guests. He was purposefully energized having realized an ambition he had quietly harbored for many years, the joy of his eldest son's marriage to an Onitsha native!

I took my daughter with us to the wedding and to my pleasant surprise she appeared to enjoy the experience immensely, meeting many relatives and her grandfather for the first time. She played excitedly with the dogs, goats and turkey near the tree, playfully planted from seeds from his finished orange, in the rich fertile soil in our compound, by my very reflective younger brother Amechi on a similar youthful visit. She was particularly excited to meet granddad's goats. We could never reveal that Beanie, her favorite, was our dinner on our last night.

We would not have my father's purposeful guidance available for our next family gathering in

OYIBOS

Onitsha. My Aunt Josephine at my father's burial told tales of how he would take her to school on the crossbar of his bicycle. She however was not a keen student despite my father's gallant efforts to encourage her to attend. Father died in Onitsha from a massive stroke two days before Christmas in 2004, the same year as the great Tsunami. He had months earlier traveled to Europe and America to spend several months at a time with each of his children and their respective families. He stayed with my sister, and my English brother-in-law, Brian (a coal-miner's son from gritty Newcastle in northern England), in the rural banking belt near London. When he married Chinwe (Patricia), Brian embraced Onitsha and us. The depth of Brian's love struck me; he actually travelled to Onitsha to ask under native custom and law for the hand of my sister. He was eager to learn our customs and to follow all aspects of Onitsha nuptials, much to my sister's consternation. Although, equally to his credit, he spoke candidly about aspects of Onitsha and Nigerian culture he did not like. He particularly liked his new respectful status and entitlements as the eldest among his brother-in-laws. His openness won over my mother, father, and sister.

While in New York, father waited for me to arrive home. I was usually exhausted after a trying day at work. He talked eagerly late into the night over a glass of Johnny Walker Black recounting tales of his life, and alas, only some of his many adventures. In hindsight I think he was saying his goodbyes and knew he did not have long to live. It was around six in the morning when I received the call. The tears came fast. Nothing prepared me for this moment and the profound sense of loss and numbing grief that followed. He was parking his beloved Volvo against doctor's orders outside my Aunt Josephine's house where he was

The Burial

delivering his customary hand reared free-range Christmas turkeys. One of our houseboys who sounded the alarm bell but to no avail accompanied him, father was pronounced dead on arrival at the hospital. I was glad that we had had an opportunity to spend quality time so close to his death. Dropping him off at JFK, I told him he should visit again the following summer, but I saw in his eyes that something was not quite right. It was a strange goodbye, from someone who knew he was not coming back but did not want to tell me. He was no doubt concerned that I would be needlessly worried. I think he probably knew his health was beyond repair and that death was beckoning. I wish he had told me how bad his heart ailment was because it would have made our time even more poignant. There was also much about his life I still needed to learn about and understand. If I had known this was to be his last journey, I would have taken more time off work to be with him.

Father's burial in February 2005, was an emotionally intense cultural experience, which made me realize how connected he was to Onitsha even in death. There were so many things he had urged us to do ahead of his death, the significance of which became apparent with his passing. He urged us, his sons, to be initiated into the masquerades, which perform dances at ceremonies marking rites of passage. Only with father's death did I realize that without our participation in these masquerades his burial as a titled Ozo man could not proceed smoothly. Burials, unlike funerals are much more of a celebration of a man or woman's life and involved the Udo clan in every aspect of the five day ceremony which included the first burial or burial of the corpse of the deceased, and the second burial which involved the symbolic burial or release of the person's soul. It was only when

OYIBOS

I saw the lifeless corpse that was my father's body which bore no resemblance to the energetic man I knew with twinkling eyes, that I realized the importance of the symbolism of also interring the soul to release the spirit from our own minds. The grieving process was so much more psychologically developed and seemed to me to be far more effective at healing emotional wounds than the somber funerals I had attended in England and America. I had a profound sadness I had never experienced before. It was a sadness that can only be understood by those who have lost a parent unexpectedly.

There were many events organized throughout the day and night, which involved the whole community celebrating my father's life. My mother and his third wife Florence remained secluded in our house in Umu Dei Village supported by close female relatives throughout the events but we were required to visit on several occasions during the ceremonies. Comfort predeceased my father having passed away while my sister Lauretta, her only daughter was visiting with me in New York. I dutifully assisted with finances for her funeral and burial in the compound of our main house in Onitsha. I hope there will be room for me when my time comes in the house in Umu Dei village.

Masked costumed masquerades were hired to dance and perform ceremonial rites in which family members joined together to make traditional music with whistles, flutes, drums, and other percussion instruments. We danced, as tradition required releasing the tension and stress from the sorrow of the loss. Perhaps the most poignant moment for me was the night I arrived in Onitsha with my half-brother Sammy from Lagos, and Regi called to say that our uncle Ofili (Oboli Boja) had summoned us to a family meeting in the village. He was now the head of the

The Burial

family with the death of his cousin. We entered his Obi (palace) near to my maternal grandmother's house and there gathered were about forty men, many in the dim light visibly resembling my own angular features. They were of various ages from eighteen to over ninety. These were the Udo men who had been gathered to organize and participate in the burial, including driving the hearse, digging the grave under one of the rooms in our house in the village and carrying the coffin for interment with us, Nnabuenyi's sons. My father was laid in state in the living room of our house in the village until my uncle pronounced it was time for the internment, whereupon we closed the heavy polished Iroko hardwood coffin and secured the brass-bolts. My sisters said their tearful goodbyes; I felt a lump in my throat and tears welled-up in my eyes. As tradition dictated we had placed some of his favorite things in the coffin. I put in his cherished English tea. As we lowered the casket, I pondered the Latin phrase mors vincit omnia, "Death conquers all" or "death always wins". Africa's fertile red soil cascaded from impatient shovels against the coffin; he was gone. Death had snatched the vitality and un-abiding love for life that my father had. He was an individual that was larger than life, a pioneer among his generation.

    I stood still solitary in my grief cutoff from the sea of sorrow around me. My thoughts were fixed on the heavenly ride I took with my father on the M5 bus along leafy, tree-lined Riverside Drive, some few months earlier in New York. It was a bright summer's day. The bus solemnly and respectfully zigzagged through the majestic architectural wonders of midtown Manhattan, the arty world of Chelsea and bohemian Greenwich Village, as we journeyed to take tea in the decorous surroundings of the fashionable Mercer Hotel in Soho. As he had in life, my father, Nnabuenyi, reveled in the changing landscape. The ebb-and-flow of the cosmopolitan city population was reflected in the altering make-up, every few blocks, of our fellow passengers. On our way back on the bus, dressed in signature Ibo attire, at one stop, he was oddly mistaken by a curious and excited passenger for the famous Yoruba drummer, Babatunji Olatunji. This was a simple life journey that my father enjoyed immensely.

20. Failed Dreams

> Will she always have to be on drugs? "Yes, but that is great as far as I'm concerned. Because you couldn't really live without them, you'd be in the nuthouse. Being diagnosed meant I actually had a chance of being a normal person." – Sinead O'Conner, *The Guardian* September 16, 2010.

In the paraphrased words of Coco Chanel, "I love my work and would not survive without it". Work for me is not only a means of sustenance but a necessary creative and cerebral outlet. The energy and content of my work affirms my independence of mind and body. It tells me I am alive.

IAT, like most businesses, has had its share of ups-and-downs. Through calamitous expansion during the "irrational exuberance" of the dot.com era to rapid contraction in today's more sober business environment. Back in 2000 every man, woman, and their dog seemed to think they could transform the business world overnight and in the process become insanely rich. Well, for most entrepreneurs like me, the truth was closer to the former than the latter, i.e., insane and destitute and not rich. I have often thought that doing business on Wall Street for the uninitiated, should carry a government health warning: "Danger: you are about to walk blindfolded and unaided through a minefield dotted with UXBs (unexploded bombs)". More recently, the firm's fortunes have paralleled those of my personal life.

It took years for me to make sense of what was wrong. Why our lives were a daily hell. Now I will tell you what I went through to get there. I will attempt to take you through my harrowing voyage, from not knowing to knowing and the attendant confusion and anguish in-between, as well as the palpable relief and joy of actually knowing.

I met and fell in love with my girlfriend in 1993, during a period when my business fortunes were very much on the up. IAT was still a small fledgling enterprise with two employees. I had been fortunate enough to invent a financial product that provided steady royalty (annuity) income. My business model was very simple. I focused on coming-up with ideas, which big banks and their large customers needed. Rather like the way small entrepreneurs today produce iPhone applications for Apple. I was part of Wall Street's little known fringe of supporting cast cottage entrepreneurs. I was an "ideas man"; one of those financial thinkers in the background that solved large often-difficult market problems that helped banks make lots of money.

IAT favored simple, elegant, bog-standard solutions that were easy for all to understand. Unfortunately though, such transparent solutions fell-out of favor as the "Greed is good" credo gripped Wall Street. The bankers of the second Millennium favored more obscure complex products, like securitized mortgages (an olfactory popery of mortgages bundled together and sold to equally greedy investors), where fees could be hidden deep and risks obscured from trusty unwitting customers. For our efforts IAT was paid a fee each time a bank and/or its customers used the firm's products. It was a massive volume based business where fees were measured in minuscule fractions of a U.S. dollar. These fees allowed me to live comfortably but certainly not well by the exaggerated standards of New York's up-and-coming investment banking elite. I was not part of that set with a retreat in the Hamptons or Château in the South of France. I was basically content with my lot, although not without some ambition, until parenthood beckoned and my girlfriend began to question why we were not living like so-and-so mercenary Wall Street banker or lawyer.

Having serially failed in love, my father taught me that romance was apt to flounder without a solid foundation, and that reckless pursuit of love left one gravely exposed to unhappiness and possible ruin. This was sage advice I would have been wise to follow before embarking on my boy-meets-girl adventure into an unreal world I had never known.

It was at a quintessential "Breakfast at Tiffany's" New York cocktail party that my initiation into American home life began in earnest. It was a cool summer's evening. The gathering was at the rooftop penthouse of a friend-of-a-friend in midtown Manhattan. The host was the son of a scion of the Rockefeller family. The event was the kind of intimate private party that young men and young husband seeking New York women, want to be invited to in the hopes of meeting a suitable other. Fortune did not seem to be on my side that evening. I was heading down the stairs from the roof to the apartment below to exit by way of the elevator when I bumped into a pretty blue-eyed young woman with a quizzical countenance. We chatted enthusiastic. "Hello I am Gus; can I flag you a cab?" "Sure, I'm Jane," she said very deliberately in a voice with a soft Southern hint clearly having noted my own clipped English vowels. Jane possessed a feral charm which intensified my curiosity. I assumed the sad look she wore was due to the absence of her Italian poet boyfriend, who I would later find out was actually a conflicted gay man passing as straight. She seemed normal (whatever that may mean), intelligent and sober. I hailed a taxi for her but not before obtaining her phone number. "Okay, hope to see you again soon", I said as the cab speed away. I called some days later and invited her to a party I was hosting, where unfortunately, due to some bizarre mishap, the ancient lock to the front-door broke leaving guests trapped at midnight in my apartment. It is only in these distressing circumstances that you find out a person's true character. A nattily attired European guest, a young German man, who seemed the picture of sophistication, on hearing the news about the lock, disintegrated into acute panic. He seriously contemplated, rather optimistically, leaping out of the window down four floors below! Fortunately other guests were able to restrain him from his folly until a New York City locksmith was summoned, at unbelievable expense, to free thankful guests some hours later. Jane, my soon to be girlfriend appeared calmer under the circumstances than my German guest; although she later confided that she was displeased at the attention I apparently lavished on a pretty Swedish friend who was also incarcerated at the party. In any event, after this encounter, we did not see each other again for almost a year since she soon departed to Romania for eight months to conclude research work on her sociology doctorate. I did, however, receive a postcard from Romania and the rest is history shall we say.

Jane was the modern Sex in the City girl: smart, attractive, blond, and blue-eyed. Our relationship, an exercise in mad-love, was a tour de force (a feat requiring great virtuosity and strength, seemingly deliberately undertaken [by each of us] for its difficulty). Before Jane, I tended to date easy going, stylish, arty, and or cosmopolitan women, but her sparkling blue-eyes, unfamiliar Southern ways, brilliant mind, and passion persuaded me otherwise. She had an intelligence and beauty that seemed off the scale. She was a new type of woman for me. I found her fascinating, and unsettling at the same time. She was short on details which made me curious to know more about her. Each date brought with it many unexpected surprises like her horse like laugh, and the fact that she was from a military family and was estranged from her father. She became hysterical if you washed blueberries in hot water (only cold would suffice), and employment was for those stupid enough not to find intellectually rewarding and publicly supported endeavors, like being a lifelong doctorate student on a scholarship. I mistook these quirky oddities and simmering bouts of unexplained fury for the unaccustomed charms of a brilliant Southern belle. It never occurred to me for one moment that she could be emotionally unwell or even a tiny bit unhinged. After all, England where I grew up was full of brilliant eccentrics. So what if at times she seemed a bit distant and strangely detached. At other times she was clever and fun. The occasional absence of commonsense or poor judgment was a small price to pay for her entertaining company. I never doubted her sincerity and gravely underestimated her cunning. We travelled the world together and she soon became the mother of my child.

Over the intervening years I would slowly and painfully transition from unknowing to the epiphany of knowing. In the process I became ensnared in the gnawing drama that would gradually destroy our lives. I learned with time that we experienced different realities. Confused, I overheard her in hushed tones on the telephone recounting daily events in our lives to friends and even my mother, in dark venomous ways that were simply unrecognizable to me. "Yes, he doesn't buy food for me, doesn't give me money, he is having affairs, and we are moving because of his wicked sinister penchant for torturing me." It became easier not to judge once I fully understood. It was near maddening when I did not know or comprehend. One close mutual friend tells of trying to reconcile tales from Jane, by gleaning information separately from me, and stitching the pieces roughly together like a mismatched patch-quilt. It was a laborious task that few in our circles bothered or were curious enough to do. The friend, a truth-seeker, logician-philosopher and filmmaker, struggled to mesh the two accounts of our lives and was stunned by the massive gaps. It was a war of narratives. We failed to agree on even basic facts. We inhabited the same home but experienced diametrically opposed realities of identical events. This made communication on even the most mundane household matters more-and-more difficult. Ultimately day-to-day communication became impossible and at its zenith the disconnected radio silences grew longer as our lives drifted apart.

Our wrecked relationship was decidedly human and messy. We were unable to profoundly connect, as H.G. Wells said: "flame meeting flame". We recklessly fell in love, although we were opposites in almost every way possible. Fleeting passion and the naïve hope that the yawning gaps in our ill-fated relationship would somehow magically repair themselves brought us together. I ended up staying because of the birth of our daughter and a deep loving desire to be part of her upbringing. Jane knew precious little about who I really was, and the same in some ways could be said of

Failed Dreams

me. She was from an America I did not recognize, and in me, she found a paradoxical and exciting conflation, a Nigerian-English-American with an Ivy League pedigree. From the beginning, I blindly ignored alarm bells sounded by my closest friends. Each pointed out our obvious incompatibilities. On a trip to visit my college roommate Bharat in Geneva, Switzerland, some months after we started dating, Jane's first impulse on arriving was to hurriedly find a pay-phone to call an ex-boyfriend she met there while interning as a student at the United Nations. She spent a not inordinate amount of time during the short trip trying furiously to track him down which I thought a trifle insensitive since the purpose of the trip was, so I thought, to spend time together and to introduce her to one of my closest and most trusted friends. All I might add at my exclusive expense and privilege since she insisted that we stay at the plush Hotel du Rhone and not with Bharat as I normally did. I suppose she did not want to come under scrutiny or close observation from sober enquiring eyes that did not necessarily share my optimistic view of the world and my naïve belief in the innate goodness of everyone.

Prior to meeting Jane, I lived a social life, which assiduously avoided those who had no basis to understand me. Part of Jane's appeal was the fact that she took me out of familiar safe-heavens into her free cascading world. This seemed novel at the time and perhaps even exciting, but her universe was populated with incongruous characters, bottom feeders and other individuals who instinctively signaled trouble. I blindly trusted, where caution was needed, assuming Jane knew America and the American way of life better than me. My sincere belief was that Jane would have my back. We would work toward common goals. She would be my protection and counter for any blind spots I had about America and Americans. In hindsight, I suspected that Jane recognized I was ill-equipped for the profound culture shock that lay ahead, but lacked the courage of her own convictions to, either come clean and tell all, or to execute a deft James Bond hand-break-turn to freedom. Prospects of escape were further complicated for both of us once she was pregnant. Jane reluctantly agreed to move into my apartment and for me as well it was an agonizing choice to co-habit with a woman I was not altogether sure was my true soul mate in life. But the impulse to be a father and hers to be a mother dictated our fate.

On news of the pending birth of our daughter, Jane's father and three of her four sisters refused to welcome me into their family because of my race. Jane's jolly, chain-smoking, and very eccentric mother, terminally ill with lung cancer, however, took to me. Mothers for whatever reason tend to like me. A Floridian pink flamingo, Bev seemed to live in a disarticulated world of her own which I attributed to her many strokes. She was a frequent visitor to our home, dropping by, often unannounced, en route to enjoy the thrills of Las Vegas or Atlantic City. Bev was also nocturnal and on occasion I would wake to find her in the darkness standing mysteriously at the foot of our bed. In this vein, she called me repeatedly at work to tell me incorrectly that Nigeria was at war and that we shouldn't attend my brother's wedding in Onitsha. Jane shared some of these curious traits. For example, she did not bother to tell me about phone calls from my aunt Franca who, like her mother, was in the throes of lung cancer and was understandably keen to have the support of her only nephew in America. Nor did she find it convenient or necessary to tell me pointed details about her. Like, for example, that she was previously married to a man who apparently was incarcerated for drug dealing! She never lied as such, but this allergy to transparency in the relationship was sobering, shockingly alarming, and upsetting. Jane brushed-off her marriage and divorce as a colossal youthful misunderstanding.

It was at Bev's in her pastel colored flower filled room in a Naples, Florida hospice, ten-years into our relationship, that I met my putative father-in-law, the grandfather of my children. We were all gathered solemnly around Bev's deathbed to hear her last wishes. Jane's four sisters and her father crowded around the bed and listened attentively to her weakened soft rasping voice, in what were Bev's few remaining lucid hours of life. Bloated with a cocktail of pain killing medication including morphine, and with an array of tubes dangling from her body, Bev's piercing blue eyes seemed at peace and reconciled to death. She always said: "Growing old sucks!" Before her death, Bev shared a morphine-induced hallucination with us. "It was fabulous; I was on a beach attended by naked buff young men with silver trays loaded with heavenly delights." "God's nectar", she said with a mischievous smile. She kept her sense of fun until the end.

Bev's sober last wishes included that her husband, Hank, should forgive her daughter and embrace his new family. It was a tragic moment. Bev wanted Hank, her estranged "knuckle-headed spouse" to share the joy she had had with us and especially with her darling granddaughter Isabel, on whom she doted. I was not sure of what to make of Hank, a man who seemed intelligent but yet refused to accept his granddaughter solely because her father was African and black. Such was Hank's animus to my relationship with his daughter, that he did not set eyes on his beautiful and brilliant granddaughter for the first ten-years of her life. As a former military officer who grew up in the segregated south, my union with his daughter was from all accounts, too much for Hank to accept.

Amidst the grief of Bev's death, our relationship lost altitude fast. Work, meanwhile, continued to deteriorate, going from bad to worse as the embers of the coming financial crisis began to smolder. Nothing was going right. My difficult home life made it difficult to manage work and work made it harder to manage a challenging home life. I mourned Bev's passing; she was the only person in Jane's family that extended a warm Yankee welcome to me. The plunge in our relationship accelerated once Jane's family members, supposedly now reformed, pressed themselves after a decade of near absence, into our lives. They behaved like long-lost relatives newly found, assuming the past had never happened.

Relaxing at the Naples Hyatt while we were visiting Bev, one of Jane's sisters arrived and shouted out to me, amused and smiling amid a crowded poolside, "I love a black man in a bathing suit!" It was regrettably typical of the insensitive behavior that pushed me away from them. They let me know in no uncertain terms, that America was their birth right not mine, the fact that I was an American too, although with a different story, was not of any consequence to them. They saw only "black", a "foreigner", and made few sincere attempts to actually know me. The void between us was a chasm deeper than the Grand Canyon. More profound than anything I had experienced growing up in England. Jane clearly found her family's behavior embarrassing and apologized on more than one occasion. I could see why she might

Failed Dreams

have felt conflicted and even uncomfortable in the company of certain members of her family. One sister in a misguided attempt to connect talked of the uplifting virtues of American slavery for black slaves, while their father droned on about all the black people he had met in his life, while mimicking, to my consternation, the Chinese waiter at the restaurant. It was as if people of color had not existed until I transgressed into their world. Not surprisingly, archconservative broadcaster, Rush Limbaugh, was required viewing among family members. All of this reinforced the sense that I had made a terrible mistake. I was very far out of bounds. There was no frame of reference to understand this particular alien American culture and monstrous mindset. I could not have imagined such a bigoted dysfunctional family. I was exposed, vulnerable, and trapped. I found myself subjected to buffeting tension; a raw ugly visceral racism, which by definition rejected me and my children by dint of our hue. After Bev's death, the harder they pushed to come in, the more I recoiled from their unrecognized and profound ignorant slips between cup-and-lip.

There were family interactions in Florida before Bev's death; Hank was absent from all of them. For Jane's family, a fun indulgence for my eight year-old in my absence, was taking her to fire rifle rounds at human shaped targets at the police gun range. Bev, her grandmother, had bequeathed her a pump action shotgun; so much for enjoying Florida's natural beauty. Not even watching The Beverly Hillbillies in Nigeria as a child could have prepared me for this surreal psychodrama.

Jane's idiosyncratic, sometimes manic, and erratic behavior went unnoticed by most outside. I witnessed days when she struggled with depression, inexplicably bursting into tears repeatedly at-the-drop-of-a-hat. She seemed in despair and was irritable, impulsive, and agitated. There were many highs and lows. One day I came home early from work, and found the parents of a child in my daughter's daycare carting-off our furniture. I asked, "What's going on?" She said, "I am giving away furniture." This was all news to me, since the furniture was already earmarked for various rooms. New alarm clocks I bought some days earlier and a weighing scale she purchased for my birthday were heaped mysteriously in the trash. On other days, I returned from work to find the apartment filled with idle girlfriends luxuriating on champagne and gourmet delights to relieve the tedium of their days, while I toiled later-and-later at the office to fund the indolent life style I could not afford but was witnessing vicariously. Such was her state that I was even bizarrely accused of being romantically involved with a woman who was dead! The friend in question was a wonderful antipodean designer with her own fashion label, who had tragically succumbed to bone cancer after a long illness. Occasionally I would be invited belatedly to a restaurant where Jane was wining and dining with her favored girlfriends, expressly to come and pick-up the tab. Her friends seemed to have the impression that I was independently wealthy, or perhaps was the son of some immensely rich far-flung potentate in darkest Africa. Few appreciated that they were drinking our weekly grocery money, and the budget for my daughter's schooling. Jane had an idle doctorate, vanishing confidence, unfinished resume, babysitter, cleaning lady whose pay she occasionally pocketed, and an exhausted bemused partner, me. I waited in vain for signs of change. She had still not responded to my marriage proposal after nearly a decade of living together and showed no interest in having more children, which I desperately wanted.

    To me Jane seemed to have everything, a caring partner, nice home, and a beautiful daughter. The reality was more sobering; a body that found her emotionally exhausted, agitated and immobilized. She buried truth behind a facade of lies, secrets, and denial. With Bev's death, there was no one left to confide in about her mood lapses. Bev had urged me not to let Jane self-medicate, (binge-drink gin to mask her depression) and to seek-out help for her. My strained superficial relationship with Jane's father and sisters and their own states of denial ruled out any help from them. The few friends she had, members of her cocktail-club who siphoned our stretched household budget, seemed equally unwilling to accept the truth. Even three separate rounds of couples counseling failed to right our relationship, although one therapist was astute enough to recognize that Jane was depressed. Naively, I blindly attributed this to the loss after eighteen-months of the only professional job she held during our thirteen-year relationship, despite her doctorate in sociology and teaching experience.

    Few knew of the unexplained disappearances, disengagement from her surroundings, and the blank expression in her gaze, particularly when she was stricken with depression. On such occasions Jane withdrew to sleep for prolonged periods whether day or night blinds and door closed in our bedroom. I pondered if she was bipolar like her sister. I took succor in the discovery that many depressed mothers manage to raise children successfully, their tattered relationships with their long suffering partners notwithstanding. I for my part increasingly buried my head in my work, which was becoming more challenging as financial markets began to implode around the world. I longed for the Saturdays spent alone with my daughter, as Jane had mandated, although she even undermined that arrangement when it suited her purpose.

Jane sought to conceal her second pregnancy during the winter months under baggy sweaters. I thought to myself, "Did she seriously think that I had not noticed the pronounced change in her form, gate, and frequent bathroom visits?" Such was our estrangement, that thoughts even crossed my mind that perhaps she was carrying another's child, which might explain her curious behavior. Eventually, after almost five months, when she could no longer even remotely conceal the pregnancy, Jane told me. "Gus, I am pregnant". This was the first exchange we had had in many months. In contrast to the unexpected surprise of our first pregnancy a few months into our courtship, I was prepared and immediately elated. I had long given up on having a sibling for our wonderful daughter who was born almost ten years earlier. As she said the words, I remembered the sad and unfortunate tale my father had told many years earlier about the wife with postpartum depression. I hoped dearly that the birth of our son would right the path of our relationship, but the irreversible decline continued and to some extent her depressive episodes became even more acute.

Whatever was going on for Jane seemed to place me at the epicenter of a great deal of negative attention. She sought to exclude me in every activity related to the birth and care of our son, to the extent that I was not even allowed to give him a bath or to put him to sleep as I had done for our daughter. I was reduced to the kindness of our young live-in Brazilian babysitter, who Jane brought home one day unannounced, to have access to my child. As the inevitable separation drew closer, hugely manipulative and keen to be seen as the victim, Jane ruthlessly played to the worst prejudices of those around her. She demonized me as a male Rat. I was cast as an angry black man with all its ugly pejorative connotations, which summon images of the O.J. Simpson case. Interestingly, Bev had some years earlier taken to calling my West African office colleague named O.T., O.J., despite being repeatedly corrected. Like Comfort, Jane fled early one morning in haste with the children, but unlike Comfort, sent two bemused and very polite New York police officers to serve protection orders against me as a violent drunken monster! Like my father witnessing the actions of the hooligans who tossed bricks through our glass door, I could not have imagined in my wildest dreams that Jane would descend so low. There was no civility or fair play here, just naked, raw, numbing anger and aggression, which revealed itself from time-to-time with the depression. I witnessed the efficacious wheels of American justice coming into play. The courts to which I was summoned, being all too familiar with this form of despicable trickery, and perhaps the effects of depression too, acted swiftly the next morning to dismiss the sham that was being orchestrated. Jane was told to vacate the apartment, which was under contract for sale and due to close to forestall imminent foreclosure. I was house rich and cash poor, the emblematic poverty deluxe of the new Millennium. I was granted immediate access to my home and children. Jane moved to the brownstone home of a naïve upwardly mobile couple, prone to vulgar ostentation and with a passion for neo-liberal causes, whom I knew through a mutual acquaintance. Before Jane's departure, the brownstone owners deemed it appropriate to cash a meaningful check written from me to Jane, (we had separate bank accounts and a joint-account for household expenses) to pay her mounting credit card and student loan arrears. Why she was borrowing was beyond me since I paid all household bills while Jane drained our joint account. The check cashing by the brownstone owners was done without my prior knowledge and the whereabouts and use of the monies are still unexplained. The brownstone owner's spouse defended these unethical and deceitful actions, ironically I thought, since he was a litigation lawyer at a major law firm, as customary practice among married "American" couples! He must have thought that I was born yesterday or freshly off the proverbial banana boat. I pointed out that dodgy practices that pertain in his household were not welcome in mine. This was borderline criminal activity as he of all people should know. Panicked and defensive as we stood talking on the street, he denounced me as "hysterical" and took to standing guard outside with his dog when I came to their Harlem brownstone to pick up my children. They became for a brief while Jane's new best friends until reality set-in and their welcome mat wore-out. Itinerant, Jane then planted herself with my children in Central Harlem.

  Jane had taken every opportunity to publicly humiliate me. It was not a pleasant situation to be in, and I wonder now how: a) I had allowed myself to get into such a destructive relationship, and b) how I endured the pain and humiliation for so long. This experience taught me the importance of not putting yourself in harm's way. In America, despite what TV commercials tell you, it is not sufficient to assume with hard work and goodwill that all will be peachy. This was not the family life I had dreamed of in America. There were no longer any playful moments to look

Failed Dreams

forward to, like evenings out with friends, or eating popcorn with our daughter while watching DVD's together as a family. The malady of depression had taken over our lives and like a tornado, tore apart everything in its wake. At the same time the financial firestorm wreaked havoc with my business intensifying discord in the household.

It was against this backdrop of my wrecked relationship that I elected to slowly return the firm to its successful roots as a small nimble and innovative business with a low cost base. My little cottage business had expanded too rapidly and like the mythological Greek character, Icarus, the sun's rays seriously singed the firm's wings. The firm plunged down to earth with a hard bump, propelled by my home problems and the broader global financial malaise. To make matters worse, an internal coup was on the boil among feuding members of our intrepid team unable to agree on the direction for the firm and its products. IAT was fast drifting out of control and was starting to look like the Shearson Lehman I had left behind. Watching the travesty unfold I was keenly aware that the firm's intellectual property resided not in our PC's or indeed in the addled minds of the various aspirants for command, but like Mozart, in the quiet and calm confines of my cranium. This was a lesson learned from my days in England at Wessex Gardens, where some foolishly assumed, that pupils who spoke no English were dim, and therefore unlikely to best them in exams.

The purpose of having a team was to better leverage my inventive talent. This seemed lost on a good number of the firms newly acquired managers. We had too many plodding chiefs and not enough smart motivated foot soldiers. Some in the ranks seemed bent on destroying the nimbleness that made IAT unique. Instead they wanted to turn the firm into yet another ponderously dull Wall Street machine with layers of warring factions driven by greed and petty office politics. This contradicted everything that was dear to me having been taught early in life that harmony was paramount and that apportioning of blame and disharmony was bad. I have since learnt in America that some measure of conflict can be healthy within confines and rules accepted by all parties. Eventually the firm was reduced to two consultants and me. I swore to return to the prudent fundamentals on which I had founded the company. While at home my separation became a reality. I was free from my daily torment at home and at work.

As with the development and manufacturer of life saving pharmaceuticals or complicated big ticket items like aircraft, where there is zero scope for error, I came to realize that the reason many new financial products fail to make it to market is that it is not an easy thing to perfect new products. New products often take lots of time, lots of work, and lots and lots of money, although admittedly as we saw in the early days at IAT, if successful, investment in new innovative products can be very rewarding. The attendant risks nonetheless particularly in the financial services industry are huge as demonstrated by the collapse of Bear Stearns, Lehman and other firms. This was precisely why IAT's original legacy business model was so powerful since it required not much more than plain old fashioned intellectual capital and minimal monetary capital other than that required for rent and money to keep phones, computers, internet connections, and body-and-soul together. All other services were appropriately outsourced. Products were prudently launched only once indications of interest were in place from players necessary for its success. These parties generally stood to gain greatly from its success. These experiences were far removed from my upbringing in Nigeria and England. Despite my Harvard linage, I learned the rules of the game in America the hard way.

Although, innovation and risk taking remains one of the bedrocks of capitalism, I now understand why the financial industry is locked into recycling old products (some gravely flawed, e.g., securitized mortgages and CDOs) where development costs have already been sunk and amortized. Nevertheless, despite failing to extend my vision beyond the firm's core competency, like most successful entrepreneurs I've tried to learn from my mistakes while keeping faith with my own genius to deliver. In rebuilding my focus has been on a handful of core companies and bank clients. The goal is to gain back the firm's niche magic and its ability to strike the right balance between short-term and long-term imperatives. Emphasis once again is on quality and satisfying client needs based on what we do best and into the bargain avoiding the pitfalls of The Wall Street rat-race and herd mentality. The firm now considerably scaled-back through fiscal attrition is once more taking reasoned tactical gambles in areas where the banks are unwilling or unable to compete; usually because of their short-term horizons and the absence of scale consistent with the quarterly discipline of public markets. Bank's today have little time for fiddly business niches but are quick to latch-on if those niches can be made to scale with handsome returns. My job at the helm most importantly remains to fulfill existing opportunities and to continue to dream big for our investors while keeping my social scruples alive.

Better acquainted with today's brawny mode of business in the financial sector, IAT should be better equipped to survive and strive. Fortunately, having incubated the firm's next new thing in my cranium and having hopefully learnt from the hard lessons from the past to protect intellectual property, I think we have our next game changing mousetrap; an audacious and ambitious project which if adopted by the market could do much to relieve the global "Credit Crunch". The global economy is worrisome and the financial sector continues to struggle; all ripe conditions for our product. The product after almost a decade of development and alignment of interested players necessary for its success is ready and scheduled for launch. Time will tell if IAT Version 3.0 is a success and if we can stay the course with timely relevant products that serve real needs. I have now graduated from my grueling twenty-five year apprenticeship in the intricacies and vagaries of the high-octane world of American capitalism. Now back to my private life.

Life having been temporarily broken and my honor tested, recovery from my separation for me and my children is paramount. "You can't play with the honor and dignity of someone", as Jack Lang, the French socialist minister of culture once said. The biggest challenge for me about separation is being away from my children and not being able to see them as often as I used too. The family court system alas is still tilted toward women in these matters, although society has evolved beyond traditional gender roles. I was under the naïve assumption that joint and or shared custody would be the norm. Instead the system requires mind-numbing jousting and financial ruin before commonsense prevails, that is, if you are lucky.

Failed Dreams

Family court is like living Kafka in vivid color and stereo in a concrete jungle, with couples screaming, children playing and crying, dithering social workers, and lawyers at each other's throats one moment, and the next, swapping war stories about their GOYARD handbags and vacations in Europe, as the cash register rings, Ka-Ching! Meanwhile the unresolved misery of their clients continues unabated. I am equally at a loss why anyone in possession of his or her faculties would elect the Byzantine court system as a venue to resolve a break-up, however complicated. Family court in New York, entails spending dreary frustrating hours witnessing the sorrows of others, now your peers, while listening to Oyibos "blowing grammar" (hot air in Nigerian vernacular), taking themselves too seriously often without the slightest hint of basic native intelligence. You are left feeling vulnerable, gravely aware, as your name and character are dragged through the mud by opposing counsel, that idiotic rulings by countless so called experts and legal professionals could ruin the lives of your children and even more dramatically, see you confined in a federal facility. Having been raised in a household where both parents were for all intense and purposes separated for much of my growing up, I have colossal empathy for what my children must be going through. Children often witness and experience traumatic filial events, as I had, that are hard to distill and to comprehend particularly when families are imploding or disintegrating. These traumatic events are not easily shared and may take years to understand and reconcile, which can be harrowing particularly at a time when a child's own formative sense of identity and loyalties are taking shape. Although to the credit of my parents we were never used as a wedge in their own marital conflagration. Remarkably, both parents went very far to ensure that we had access, as far as I can recall, to each parent as we wished.

There are things in my relationship with Jane looking back that now seem obvious. Stuff I failed to realize to my own detriment. Often tiny details, like her not leaving the apartment for days. More attention to the genesis of these telltale signs might have elicited greater understanding and compassion on my part. Perhaps, against all imponderable odds, may have even salvaged our relationship. Jane paradoxically yearned for a conventional American home life. By definition, given my foreign birth, I felt this was not only improbable but also flat-out impossible without rewriting our respective histories. She frequently yelled at me, "Loser!" "Be a Man!" How to play the role of the idealized "[American] Man" was something I could not fathom, just like I have never been able to eat peanut butter and jelly sandwiches. The combination for me was contradictory. I did not realize I was supposed to bring home the bacon, and stay out of the way, quietly deferring on household matters. We were to have our polarized domains; Jane's the home, and me the office. And never the twain shall meet. The "bacon" ideally was to be delivered in ever-larger quantities and spent in line with the unspoken dreams and aspirations conjured up, in my absence, at home by my melancholy and emotional Southern girlfriend. What Jane and I failed to realize was that I did not have the faintest clue about my assumed role in that very particular reality TV show. Nor did I have a desire to play a role, which as written, appeared from my unique vantage point, to have inadvertently omitted me and understated my Co-Star's role.

Failed Dreams

Choosing the right partner is one of the most important things in our lives. It is partly a matter of luck and timing "but should not be left to careless chance," as my father had cautioned. Father told me, "It takes time to know someone," a statement I did not fully appreciate until now. I had empathy for Jane once I knew and better understood the source of her anguish and how it colored our relationship. Distinguishing between the subtle boundaries of the diabolical mischief of a genius and the psychotic effects of ebbing chemical imbalances brought on by depression was a challenge. With hindsight, I wish in some ways I had had my epiphany at the start. This would have given me a valuable insight into the intimate realms of Jane's mind and the depression I witnessed. Not to mention the despair caused by her transient journey as a troubled and cloistered military child adapting constantly to shifting friends and locations. This was a life story left largely untold to me.

I wanted to comprehend Jane's noble quest for inner peace, to prevail over depression. In the twilight of our relationship, I watched without understanding as she struggled to progress from pills to a regime of better nutrition and diet with regular exercise, regulation of stimulants like caffeine and alcohol, and I hoped and suspected costly therapy. The latter, might in part explain the black whole in our joint account, which was always never enough. Interestingly mother, bless her, steadfastly maintained that Jane was not ill as such but burdened with the afflictions of life's routine's that can weigh heavily on women and hamper individual fulfillment with consequential gloom. I suspect there is more than a kernel of truth in her observations. Nevertheless, the stigma and taboo of mental illness or perhaps the depression itself prevented the openness and honesty that was vital for the survival of our relationship. Greater lucid understanding from both of us of the moment I think would have resulted, in a happier ending, or at least an amicable separation. Depression won the day. Her struggle will no doubt continue and one hopes Jane will triumph in the battle to control the carnage depression can cause. I certainly see our relationship in a fresh illuminating way. I've learned to see Jane with new understanding. My unexpected but instructive insight into the workings of a brilliant but intermittently faulty mind and the Blitzkrieg it can cause for owner and bystanders alike were irreversibly life changing. It opened new vistas and underscored the fact that Jane and I are forever bound through our children. Although our lives are now free from the mutual daily anguish of living together. Healing with time might usher the thawing of relations, as I witnessed with Comfort and my father.

Boarding the jet to freedom at Ikeja Airport in 1966, I could not have imagined that I would end up living among Oyibos (Europeans) for so long in such close and intimate terms as I have shared with you here, building a life first in England and then here in America, as an American. In doing so, I failed in my quest to find my American dream of domestic bliss. Instead I learned how not to judge, which is incredibly difficult if you are afflicted with an English upbringing. I might add also that never was I tempted to follow my father's path into the polygamist world of an Onitsha traditionalist. On the contrary, my experience convinced me that one partner at any one time, was more than enough for any man or woman to cope with, above all in America! Ironically, despite my early childhood traumas, I had no sense at all that the world was a bad place. A potential Pandora's box for New York's therapist community no doubt. My sometimes-surreal life experiences however did not obscure the emigrant promise of a happy ending, a silver lining in this third stanza of my journey from my birthplace to New York. This silver lining was realized in an unexpected and spectacular way, through the birth of Isabel and Nicholas, our two beautiful, smart, and adorable children.

Today, materially poorer, but faculties, health, dignity, and soul intact, and wealthier with my experiences, I am now free to embark on my next journey.

The End

EPILOGUE

Onitsha

I started my journey a in distant culture light-years from New York, surviving my twin and the storms of Nigeria's brewing civil war to navigate Britain's conflicting culture and eventually to land in Cambridge which served as my bridge into the United States and becoming an American. Having had the moxie to make it to America, the challenge now is fulfilling my American Dream. My initial fanciful dreams of America and Americans have been brought down to earth with a resounding bump. I've learned hard lessons, some very painful indeed. Like many newcomers, I have had to reassess the America that is separate from that of our dreams. I've had to revisit different places in my journey including friendships that failed time honored tests of understanding, loyalty, and support. I've swept out unaccustomed superficial fluff that can overwhelm those new to America. People who like me were not fully versed in American ways as how to discern what and who is fleeting and those truly founded on deep bedrock. One can only survive in isolation for so long without these basic skills of how to escape the shackles of heady American impulses that can send you skyrocketing one moment and to economic oblivion the next. My remarkable experience of becoming a U.S. citizen, has taught me the subtle difference between becoming American and being American.

The birth of my daughter Isabel and my son Nicholas ten years apart are perhaps the single most important events in my life. These events were doubly profound to witness having survived my twin. The poignancy of the moment of their births was underlined by the fact that Isabel was born on the same day as me, highlighting a curious circularity.

Nicholas symbolically, was also born on the sixteenth, albeit in a different month and year. I am not given to superstition but these coincidences do give me cause for pause to thank our ancestors and my Chi (God). My children are a gift and an immense source of joy and pride. Isabel like many Udo women is intelligent, sensitive, beautiful, and wise beyond her years. Nicholas like his grandfather is playful, smart, handsome, sporty, and confident. Kind spirited, gifted, and talented, I could not wish for more other than to hope they will grow to marry happily with children and look after me, and their mother, in our separate and respective old age. This of course implies that they will inherit the old country sense of respect and care for the aged particularly those to whom they are related.

I hope my children will be successful in reconciling the conflicting pulls of their cultural heritage. I want them to feel comfortable and connected however tenuously to their multicultural roots. I realize that my own life when compared with my parent's was very different and that the lives of my children in America will be equally different from mine. On my side, it is my hope that I will be sensible enough to give Isabel and Nicholas the needed room to view their tri-cultural Nigerian-English-American heritage from their respective vantage points. To take from each, elements, as I have, that will enrich their own lives. I have not been as diligent, as my parents were, in teaching them Onitsha-Ibo, and sadly my own speaking skills are waning with each year away from daily discourse in Ibo. This is a huge regret for me because it clearly limits their access to exploring their family connections in Nigeria and roots in Onitsha. I have worked on-the-other-hand to explain the complexities of family relationships, tradition, and custom much more so than my parents found it necessary to do. I've also tried to give Isabel and Nicholas an insight into how family and environment molded me. As well as generational characteristics and personality traits shaped by DNA. Isabel is well travelled having been to Africa, Asia, the Caribbean, and Europe. She is equipped to understand and appreciate different cultures and social mores in a way that many of her peers simply will not. This brings its own unique pleasures and burdens. Unlike me, however, having grown up in America, she is attuned to the country's pulse in a way that I will never be, even after almost a quarter of a century living continuously in America. Both she and Nicholas delight in correcting my Queen's English (i.e., as in the Queen of England not the borough in New York), and they will see and experience America in a very different way from me, which I appreciate and welcome.

My fissure from their American born mother, in a peculiar way, provides an opportunity for my children to appreciate the heritage of both parents more fully from a distance. It allows them to establish that vital connection to important cultural anchors that shape where we come from and how we tackle the world we find ourselves.

Like many parents I worry about the future of my children, especially for Nicholas as a bright young man of color in a sometimes-hostile world. Like many Americans I am deeply troubled by the frightening statistics of incarnated black men and how race can lead to brutally and savagely curtailed opportunity in America. It seems even seemingly successful individuals are not immune to capricious slings and arrows of outwardly disproportionate misfortunate, President Obama notwithstanding. The disgraceful heckling of President Obama while addressing the nation by an elected politician and the hateful and shocking cover of New York Magazine (September 28, 2009, edition) have done little to disabuse me of my concerns.

    My own experiences have not served to temper my concerns for Nicholas's future especially now his mother has elected for reasons known only to her to fix him and Isabel in the rough and tumble environs of Central Harlem with all its attendant challenges. I can only conclude perhaps that it is some misguided sense of trying to connect with "The Black" within herself. I can assure you, however, that she will not find many American-English-Nigerians in the neighborhood to help affirm the identity of my children that she is so keen to strip and dilute. As I have learned in my years in America, you do not have to go to Harlem to have your identity affirmed as that of a person of color and culture. I recall merrily crossing the road one sunny afternoon opposite Saks department store on Fifth Avenue in New York, and out-of-the-blue being accosted by a young and very aggressive police officer, who apparently felt it necessary to single me out from the predominantly white throng of people crossing the road for a ludicrous in-your-face hands-on-revolver caution about not crossing the road against the red traffic light. It is hard to escape race in America because race will often find you by dint of the color of your skin. Such incidents and others I encountered at Fairway, Lehman, and elsewhere make me reflect, perhaps cynically, on the fortunes of the fearsome local Nigerian rulers Onyeama and the legendary Jaja of Opobo who questioned the status quo of British rule and their right to move freely and to conduct trade and commerce unmolested in their own land. They paid ultimately with their lives. The remnants of deep-seated prejudices, discrimination, and hate still linger in America. I fear that only time and the inextricable drift toward an inclusive multicultural society, which shifting demographic imperatives portend, will help eradicate the past.

Being a hopeless optimist, I have never been particularly good at, nor have I found it, perhaps foolishly, of paramount importance in my life to safeguard against legions of backsliders and backstabbers who are quick to exploit the weakness of others in a tremendously competitive America. To this end, I would like to teach my children to be alert to duplicity and wary of dubious emissaries, faux bonhommes, bearing gifts of Trojan horses. Passing on the importance of sincerity in life, with eyes wide open, is vital to me, which does not necessarily preclude rubbing elbows and being enmeshed in the fast paced and sometime hazardous world of the Oyibos. These are all good and desirable things in life, basic forgotten decent commonsense, dare I say, American values.

I tell my children that: "Nwa Eze edi fu naba" (a child from a royal family is not lost in a foreign land).

The strong and sometimes forgotten pulse of my Onitsha heritage still flicker particular with the annual month long New York visit of my mother. While she is here, we call relatives and family friends drawn to America in search of freedom and opportunity. The same routine prevailed when my father was alive. For those few fleeting weeks together we speak Ibo and celebrate where we came from and eat pounded-yam and garri with Egusi soup made from spinach, palm oil, and ground watermelon seeds. We remember remnants of our lives before and after our destiny were irreparably altered by Nigeria's civil war. We talk about England, curtailed, as well as realized opportunities. On the occasions we manage to gather other kinfolk, like my father's London salons, we break bread, and reminisce, less so though about Onitsha, and more so about Nigeria at large. This is reflective of changing generations and our subtly waning Onitsha ties. These occasions nevertheless keep the foundations of my roots watered and alive.

My culture shock has left me with some ambivalence but mostly hope. Today's America is becoming progressively anesthetized lacking the vibrancy I found when I first arrived in Cambridge three decades ago. The moral and ethical turpitude that caused the recent financial crisis is breathtaking, as is the lack of remorse one encounters among those at the epicenter of so much pain for many Americans and other citizens around the world. I was not too surprised to see many greedy, unlettered, unethical, and unimaginative bankers tumble along with their institutions including Lehman Brothers, in the financial crisis or "Credit Crunch" of 2007-8. I was surprised however that few of these bankers actually ended up in jail.

Like the Hobbesian scene of bygone days at Murtala Muhammed International Airport, unchecked by co-opted and compromised regulators, some asleep at the wheel, these bankers and financiers pushed America's tradition of winning and competition beyond all reasonable and ethical bounds into the realm of unbridled greed. The "Greed is good" credo of the New Millennium is still alive and well on Wall Street. Like Olympians, bankers have a singular winning goal. That goal is to make pots of money; don't be fooled otherwise. This is something that regulators and lawmakers still don't fully comprehend. Wall Street's "Too Big to Fail" doctrine effectively socializes risk and allows bankers super-sized upside, which means you and I have the ultimate responsibility as taxpayers for the inevitable mistakes of greedy bastards on Wall Street. The bonus reward system that pays bankers bonuses whether their institution makes money or not is clearly another disincentive to behave responsibly. These are children left unsupervised in a sweet (candy) shop, and I frankly find it hard to understand why people are surprised that jars are broken and sweets are consumed without any restraint or compunction. Bankers have been placed in a position to hold global economies hostage with ice-cool revolvers held to the heads of governments. Under these asymmetric conditions, which are antithetical to capitalism, there is little incentive for Wall Street to behave and every incentive for bankers to misbehave. Unlike the communal balance I was taught in Onitsha-Ibo culture, self-interested shortsightedness reigns supreme and is the norm on Wall Street more so than any other time that I recall in my lifetime. Similarly for some firms that support the activities of these institutions, there is no noblesse oblige, "You kill what you eat". The irresponsible actions of avaricious bankers came very close to precipitating the demise of American capitalism. It certainly derailed my livelihood along with those of many others around the world. Like a massive earthquake their misdeeds sent tidal waves across the financial world dragging down with it the real bricks-and-mortar economy. Many innocent victims were claimed who couldn't even begin to explain what Wall Street does and what business it has destroying their lives, from Reykjavík to Lagos, the difference being that in Lagos the chief executives are being held directly accountable for their recklessness deeds.

Finding the America I signed up for at my swearing-in ceremony is part of my quest today. Then America was an exciting place to be. It was a country with a soul that was at the forefront of much of what was good for humanity. This is what led me to America, not Coca Cola or the desire for a job where I would wear a crease in my pants (trousers) and have a fat wallet in my back pocket.

Through my long journey I've learned to decipher and navigate the travails of being tri-cultural and always struggling to fit perfectly in. I no longer feel like a rootless extraterrestrial. I've come to terms with the rich and textured fabric that is my life; able to manage and play my tri-cultural Deuces, my Nigerian-British-American identity without compromising my integrity, who I am. I am a global citizen; a product of all three cultures. I relish learning more about life and dreaming the American way with a fuller understanding of what that means, i.e., without getting tricked by the monstrous America I had not known.

I intend to live my next fifty-years to its fullest in celebration of my ancestors, my children, and my journey to America.

Acknowledgements

This book came about from scrawled notes intended as a quick sketch for my children of their father's family. Those notes morphed into a manuscript as various family members and friends reminded me of events and countless tales that marked a turbulent early life and a storied adolescence and adulthood.

Some of the names in this book have been changed to protect the privacy of the individuals concerned but otherwise all names and events are real. In the early years, given my tender age, I have relied as best I could on memory and recounted, as well as reconstructed tales from family and friends.

This book would not have been possible without help, encouragement, inspiration, and contribution from my mother, my father (through his efforts at compiling a family tree before his death), my sisters, Augusta, and Patricia, and my brother Regi, my daughter Isabel who listened to an early dinner reading at a friend's house without falling asleep, unlike her much younger brother Nicholas (who was clearly uninspired by the text) and spotted some wordsmith edits, and other family members.

I received encouragement from many friends some seeking to know more about me and my family, including: Gordon Bell, Gisela Bucher, Emeka Dike, Adam Dixon, Bharat Dube, Jennifer Dworkin, Louis Edozien, Tony Emengo, Ellen Gallagher, James E. Johnson, Beth Judy, Hasan Kayali, Mde et M. Kearney (aka, Béatrice Leca and Jeffrey Kearney), Jenny Freeman, Judy Levenfeld, Antonio Maldonado Camera, Anthony Maybury-Lewis, Nancy Northup, Denise Shannon, Angie Triebe, Eve Trout and my editors Anne Dubuisson Anderson and Judy Sternlight.

Gus Udo
New York November 2010

Suggested Reading

A Friend of the Gods, by Isaac Anieka Mbanefo.
A New Palace is Born, co-edited by Jo.-Bel Molokwu and Chike Akosa.
American Notes, by Charles Dickens.
At Her Majesty's Request, by Walter Dean Myers.
Books v. Cigarettes, by George Orwell.
Britain's Top Financial Regulator Takes on Banks, The New York Times September 24, 2009, by Landon Thomas, Jr.
Darkness Visible: A Memoir of Madness, by William Styron
Democracy in America, by Alexis de Tocqueville.
Death and the King's Horseman, A Play by Wole Soyinka.
End of Empire, by Brian Lapping.
Experiment in Autobiography, by H.G. Wells.
Gabriel García Márquez: A Life, by Gerald Martin.
Groundwork of the History and Culture of Onitsha, by S.I. Bosah.
Half of a Yellow Sun, by Chimamanda Ngozi Adichie.
Here is New York, by E.B. White.
Heroes & Heroines of Onitsha, by Chike Akosa.
Home and Exile, by Chinua Achebe.
Igbo Culture and Socialization, collated by Uzoma Onyemaechi.
Incognito: The Secret Lives of the Brain, by David Eagleman
Lost in Translation, by Eva Hoffman.
Man the State and War, by Kenneth Waltz.
Moral Clarity: A Guide for Grown-Up Idealist, by Susan Neiman.
My East End, by Gilda O'Neill.

"Old Immigrants, Invisible with 'Nobody to Talk To', The New York Times August 31, 2009, by Patricia Leigh Brown.
Nigger at Eton, by Dillibie Onyeama.
Strength in What Remains, by Tracey Kidder.
The Art of War, by Sun Tzu.
The Ghost in the House, by Tracy Thompson.
The King in Every Man: Evolutionary Trends in Onitsha Ibo Society and Culture, by Richard Henderson, Yale University Press, 1972.
The Lonely Londoners, by Sam Selvon.
The Nigerian Revolution and the Biafra War, by Alexander A. Madiebo.
The Rulers of British Africa, 1870-1914, by Lewis H. Gann, Peter Duignan.
The Shortness of Life, by Seneca.
The Trouble with Nigeria, by Chinua Achebe.
Tom Brown's School Days, by Thomas Hughes.
Unaccustomed Earth, by Jhumpa Lahiri.
Why I Write, by George Orwell.
Young Converts: Christian Missions, Gender and Youth in Onitsha, Nigeria 1880-1929, by Misty L. Bastian.

Author's Biography

GUS UDO was born in Kaduna in northern Nigeria on November 16, 1959. He was raised in London and studied at Harvard College and the London School of Economics and Political Science (LSE). The author spends his time in London, Paris, and New York where he lives and works. He has two children.

This is the author's first book.

www.ingramcontent.com/pod-product-compliance
Lightning Source LLC
Chambersburg PA
CBHW031425150426
43191CB00006B/404